Equality Matters

Multilingual Matters

Breaking the Boundaries
    EUAN REID and HANS H. REICH (eds)
Child Language Disability: Volume I, II and III
    KAY MOGFORD-BEVAN and JANE SADLER (eds)
Citizens of This Country: The Asian British
    MARY STOPES-ROE and RAYMOND COCHRANE
Community Languages: A Handbook
    BARBARA M. HORVATH and PAUL VAUGHAN
Continuing to Think: The British Asian Girl
    BARRIE WADE and PAMELA SOUTER
Deaf-ability - Not Disability
    WENDY McCRACKEN and HILARY SUTHERLAND
Education for Work
    DAVID CORSON (ed.)
Education of Chinese Children in Britain and the USA
    LORNITA YUEN-FAN WONG
Emerging Partnerships: Current Research in Language and Literacy
    DAVID WRAY (ed.)
Local Management of Schools
    GWEN WALLACE (ed.)
The Management of Change
    PAMELA LOMAX (ed.)
Managing Better Schools and Colleges
    PAMELA LOMAX (ed.)
Managing Staff Development in Schools
    PAMELA LOMAX (ed.)
One Europe - 100 Nations
    ROY N. PEDERSEN
Opportunity and Constraints of Community Language Teaching
    SJAAK KROON
Parents on Dyslexia
    S. van der STOEL (ed.)
Performance Indicators
    C. T. FITZ-GIBBON (ed.)
Policy Issues in National Assessment
    P. BROADFOOT et al. (eds)
Psychology, Spelling and Education
    C. STERLING and C. ROBSON (eds)
Primary Science
    LYNN D. NEWTON (ed.)
School to Work in Transition in Japan
    KAORI OKANO
Story as Vehicle
    EDIE GARVIE
Teacher Supply and Teacher Quality
    GERALD GRACE and MARTIN LAWN (eds)
The World in a Classroom
    V. EDWARDS and A. REDFERN

Please contact us for the latest book information:
Multilingual Matters Ltd,
Frankfurt Lodge, Clevedon Hall, Victoria Road,
Clevedon, Avon BS21 7SJ, England

Equality Matters

Case Studies from the Primary School

Edited by
Hilary Claire, Janet Maybin
and Joan Swann

MULTILINGUAL MATTERS LTD
Clevedon • Philadelphia • Adelaide

Library of Congress Cataloging in Publication Data

Equality Matters: Case Studies from the Primary School/Edited by Hilary Claire,
Janet Maybin and Joan Swann
p. cm.
1. Education, Elementary–Great Britain–Case Studies. 2. Education, Elementary–Great
Britain–Curricula–Case Studies. 3. Educational Equalization–Great Britain–Case Studies.
I. Claire, Hilary II. Maybin, Janet III. Swann, Joan.
LA633.E68   1993
372.941–dc20

British Library Cataloguing in Publication Data

A CIP catalogue record for this book is available from the British Library.

ISBN 1-85359-181-5 (hbk)
ISBN 1-85359-180-7 (pbk)

Multilingual Matters Ltd

UK: Frankfurt Lodge, Clevedon Hall, Victoria Road, Clevedon, Avon BS21 7SJ.
USA: 1900 Frost Road, Suite 101, Bristol, PA 19007, USA.
Australia: P.O. Box 6025, 83 Gilles Street, Adelaide, SA 5000, Australia.

Printed and bound in Great Britain by the Longdunn Press, Bristol.

Contents

Introduction
Hilary Claire, Janet Maybin and Joan Swann 1

PART I: CHILDREN
1   'He Doesn't Like You, Miss': Working with Boys in an
    Infant Classroom
    Diane Reay 13
2   Chris Raine's Progress
    Alyson Clare 22
3   Signing in Class
    Beate Schmidt-Rohlfing 31
4   Children Who Don't Stand Out
    Lynda Yard 43
5   Working with Traveller Children
    Brian Foster, Andrew Pritchard, Siobhan, Brigid Gaffey,
    Kathleen Joyce 53
6   Looking Back: Teenage Girls' Recollections
    Sofia Choudhary, Sarah Davis, Nicola Darvill, Sheli Ullah,
    Haleema 65

PART II: CLASSROOMS AND CURRICULUM
7   Story Box
    Amar Khela and Monica Deb 77
8   Global Education For Equality
    Margot Brown 91
9   Some Equality Issues In Primary Design and Technology
    Anne Waldon 102
10 Aprons and Attitudes: A Consideration of Feminism
    in Children's Books
    Sue Adler 111
11 Assessment in Mathematics and Science: Issues for Teachers
    Anne Qualter 124
12 Assessing Humanities: Some Notes
    Pat Hughes 132
13 Assessing Language
    Joan Swann 139

PART III: WHOLE SCHOOL
14 Starting Points
    Jackie Hughes 151
15 Developing a Whole School Approach for Dealing with
    Bullying in the Primary School
    Celestine Keise 163
16 Parents and Equal Opportunities
    Ann Watson 176
17 An Equal Hierarchy
    Pete Sanders 187
18 Equal Opportunities and Sexuality
    Paul Patrick and Helena Burke 200

Biographical Details

Contributors

Sue Adler has lived in London since the early 1970s. She works in education as a librarian and part-time lecturer, combining her interests in and commitment to children, their books, and issues of equality.

Margot Brown spent many years working in inner city primary schools. It was there that she first became involved in issues of equality. She has since worked with teachers in class and on in-service courses linking equality issues and global education theories and practice.

Helena Burke is currently responsible for personal health and social education in a South London Comprehensive. She is also a tutor for initial teacher training and lectures on issues of social education. She has been actively involved in developing equal opportunities in schools since she started teaching in 1986.

Alyson Clare was head teacher at Ravenstonedale Endowed School, Cumbria, when she wrote her chapter on 'Chris Raine's progress'. With ten year's experience of primary education in the county her particular interest was in children with learning difficulties and ways of providing opportunities and support for them in the classroom situation.

Monica Deb has worked in schools across phases and is currently working as a language development teacher.

Brian Foster has been involved in Traveller Education for more than a decade and is currently the co-ordinator of the Inner London Traveller Education Team. He was the GLC's Outreach Worker for Travellers and encouraged the adoption of more positive policies towards Travellers by local authorities in London.

Jackie Hughes has been Headteacher at St George's Church of England Primary School in Birmingham since January 1990. She has over twenty years teaching experience in a variety of Birmingham schools and considerable experience in the field of promoting equal opportunities as part of good primary classroom practice and whole school management structures. She is married with a grown up family and is an ordained Minister in the Church of England.

Pat Hughes is a former primary school teacher who is now working in initial teacher training at Liverpool Institute of Higher Education. She writes primary history materials for scholastic publications and Oxford University Press.

Celestine Keise currently works as an LEA school inspector. She has responsibility for gender equality and pupil behaviour management. She has worked extensively with primary and secondary schools, with governing bodies and parents' groups in the development of whole school approaches for dealing with bullying and harassment including the production of school and LEA policies.

Amar Khela has a wide experience of teaching in schools and colleges and is currently working as an Area Coordinator with a project aimed at ensuring equal access to the curriculum for all pupils.

Paul Patrick is currently Head of Year at a South East London Comprehensive. He was a founder member of the Lesbian/Gay Teachers Group and has worked for the development of lesbian and gay issues in education since he came out in 1974. In 1990 he was presented with the Edward Carpenter Award for service to the lesbian and gay cause. He was an Advisory Teacher for equal opportunities and the pastoral curriculum in the Inner London Health Education Authority from 1984 to 1987.

Andrew Pritchard, a native of West London, spent most of the 1970s and 1980s travelling in various parts of the world. He and his partner travelled and worked for several years in a European Circus and the early education of their own children was in a mobile Circus school. Andrew has been working as peripatetic Teacher for Travellers in the West London Borough of Ealing since 1989.

Anne Qualter has been a researcher in Science and Assessment with the APU (Assessment of Performance Unit), and then at CRIPSAT (Centre for Research in Primary Science and Technology). She has been involved in the development of SATS at key stages 1 and 2, and in evaluating the National Curriculum Science. Throughout she has maintained a concern for equal opportunities in education and presently lectures on these issues at Liverpool University.

Diane Reay has taught in Inner London primary schools for eighteen years. Since then she has worked as an advisory teacher in Ealing and Islington. She is currently undertaking a research scholarship at South Bank University, investigating mothers' involvement in their children's primary school education.

Prior to taking up his current post as Senior Lecturer in Health Education at the University of North London, Pete Sanders worked for ten years as a

Primary School Headteacher. He has also done extensive work in the area of Senior Educational Management Training, and is the author of fifteen books.

Beate Schmidt-Rohlfing's interest in working with the deaf stemmed from a holiday with deaf teenagers, during which she became aware of the richness of their communication. She trained as a teacher of the deaf at Heidelberg University and worked first in Germany then in England in schools for the deaf. After many years of using the 'oral' approach, she was happy with the change to 'Total Communication', which assists in ensuring equal opportunities for the education of all deaf children.

Ann Watson, MEd, originally trained in Fine Art, and has taught in a variety of schools. She was deputy head teacher for ten years and has since left the teaching profession.

Anne Waldon became interested in equal opportunities when she taught physics in comprehensive schools. Was something wrong with the values of science, or the way it was being taught, if girls were not taking it up? She pursued this interest in primary teaching and became a science and later a technology advisory teacher. She began working for the National Curriculum Council in 1992.

Lynda Yard was the Croydon Coordinator for the National Oracy Project and is now an advisory teacher for Primary English. Listening intently to children has led to an interest in learning to listen to adults and, as Lynda Graham, she is now studying for a diploma in Person Centred Counselling.

Editors

Hilary Claire was brought up in South Africa, and left hurriedly in 1964. She has been involved in primary education in England for many years as a classroom teacher, researcher, advisory teacher and teacher educator. She now lectures in history and primary education at South Bank University. Publications include *Classroom Collaboration* (1984, Routledge) (with Phil Salmon), *We Can Stop It? A Handbook on Combating Bullying in Schools* (1992), and many articles on anti-racist and anti-sexist practice, mathematics, design technology and teaching women's history.

Janet Maybin trained as a social anthropologist and has worked for many years in the Open University School of Education, contributing to MA, undergraduate and inservice courses and packs on language and literacy. She has published several articles on children's language and has a long term interest in issues of social practice.

Joan Swann taught in secondary schools in Salford and Manchester, and now works as a lecturer in language and education at the Open University where she has contributed to several undergraduate and inservice courses and packs. Publications include *Gender Voices* (1989, Basil Blackwell) (with David Graddol) and *Girls, Boys and Language* (1992, Blackwell), as well as several articles on language and education.

The editors would like to thank Pam Powter from the Open University School of Education who assisted in the compilation of the book. She was responsible for word processing, administration and management of production of the final manuscript.

Acknowledgements

Chapter 2 'Chris Raine's Progress' has been revised and reproduced with permission from The Open University. The original version appeared in Booth, T., Swann, W., Masterton, M. and Potts, P. (eds) (1992) *Learning for all 1: Curriculum for Diversity in Education*. London: Routledge.

Grateful acknowledgement is made to the authors concerned for the reproduction of photographs and other materials in their chapters. Also to Ruth Lambourne who took the photographs on pp. 95 and 120 specially for this book, and to Mike Levers of The Open University for photographs on pp. 36 and 37.

Introduction

HILARY CLAIRE, JANET MAYBIN and JOAN SWANN

Our ideas for (and about) this book were developing at the start of the 1990s, as the Education Reform Act extended its influence in primary schools and classrooms. At the time, we were all involved in the production of Open University in-service materials for teachers. We began to share the fears of several teachers we met: that, with the need for an immediate — even urgent — response to government initiatives, continuing issues such as equal opportunities were in danger of being neglected. Certainly, a quick perusal of national curriculum documentation shows that, while there are several references to equality of opportunity, there is little discussion of what this means for classroom practice. In the nonstatutory guidance for English, for instance, we are told that in planning for speaking and listening 'the need for equal opportunities for boys and girls should receive consideration' (NCC, 1989: C4); furthermore, 'to secure implementation of the programmes of study [for English at key stage 1] schools will need to ensure that materials are varied, come from a wide range of sources, and comply with policy on equal opportunities' (NCC, 1989: B3). What such policies might look like, however, receives scant attention.

We wanted to bring together accounts of equal opportunities work, written in the main by practising teachers or others with direct practical involvement in primary education. Our aim was that these would provide ideas and suggestions that could be taken up in other schools and classrooms, but also that they would stimulate debate: after two or three decades of concern about equal opportunities issues it seems timely to reflect on what counts as effective policy and practice.

Equality of opportunity is not an easy notion: the phrase has been variously interpreted, and there will undoubtedly be disagreement about what constitutes 'good practice'. In collecting material for the book, we have tried to represent some of this diversity: we have included a wide range of topics from contributors with different perspectives on equal opportunities. Our criteria were that each chapter should be interesting in its own right; that it should offer a positive way forward on equal opportunities, while not glossing over difficulties and concerns; and that, collectively, chapters would develop and broaden the notion of equality of opportunity.

In the remainder of this introduction, we first discuss 'equal opportunities work in context' — both the broad social and political context in which equal opportunities have developed as an important issue within education and, on a local level, the need for a contextualised approach to implementing and evaluating equal opportunities initiatives. We then say a little more about the way the book is organised, and about issues that recur in different chapters.

Equal Opportunities Work in Context

Looking back, a succession of Government Acts has marked the importance of issues of class, gender, race, disability and sexuality in relation to children's educational opportunities, as Figure 1 shows. (This does not include the various Government Circulars and Acts which marked Labour's attempts to move the country towards a unified system of secondary education and the Conservatives' resistance to comprehensivisation.)

There is always a complex relationship between social change and official recognition of this through changes in national law and policy. 'Recognition' can sometimes take the form of trying to hide or reverse social changes. The diagram opposite (compiled from Statham & Mackinnon, 1991) needs to be read within the general political and social context of the period, including research trends. For instance the economic priorities in post-war Britain and the recruiting of workers from former colonies; the growing recognition of underachievement among particular groups of children; and the growth of the black civil rights movement, the women's liberation movement and the gay movement are all important to understanding the impetus behind legislation, and the manner of its implementation.

Now in the early 1990s we are experiencing a period of economic recession and wide-reaching changes following the 1988 Education Reform Act. There have been cut-backs in local authority equal opportunities work and initiatives. As we mentioned earlier, individual teachers and schools are under such enormous pressures in coping with organisational changes and the new measures of accountability, that there is a danger of equal opportunities issues being marginalised. We believe that it is particularly important at this time to record and disseminate good practice, as well as to highlight and question the inequalities perpetuated through school organisation, curriculum content or methods of teaching and assessment.

The chapters in this book are grouped under three broad headings: Children; Classrooms and Curriculum; and Whole School. In practice it has

1944 Education Act:	The first official recognition of the concept of equal opportunities within education, this Act established a unified system of free compulsory schooling for children aged from five to fifteen. Every child would therefore have the opportunity to fulfil their intellectual potential, regardless of class or economic background. Children with special educational needs were to be educated in ordinary schools wherever possible.
1966 Local Government Act:	Funds allocated (under Section 11) to local authorities to employ extra staff for education and other purposes in areas with large numbers of Commonwealth immigrants for whom special provision is required because of differences in language or customs.
1975 Sex Discrimination Act:	Sex discrimination prohibited in relation to admissions to schools, appointment of teachers (except in single-sex schools) and careers advice. Neither girls nor boys should be refused access to 'any courses, facilities or other benefits provided' solely on the grounds of their sex.
1976 Race Relations Act:	Discrimination on the grounds of race prohibited in the same areas as those identified under the 1975 Sex Discrimination Act. Positive discrimination in favour of disadvantaged racial groups only to be allowed in circumstances of special need or training.
1981 Education Act:	Following the recommendations of the 1978 Warnock Report, a new definition of special needs greatly increased the number of children involved; these children were to be educated in ordinary schools wherever possible. It became the local authority's responsibility to produce statements specifying individual children's special needs and to make provision to meet them.
1988 Local Government Act:	An amendment (Section 28) forbade local authorities to 'promote teaching in any maintained school of the acceptability of homosexuality as a pretended family relationship'.*

* The practical effect of this on schools is still unclear because of the vagueness of wording in the amendment (e.g. how 'promote' should be defined) and the onus being placed on local authorities rather than on schools.

not always been easy to decide where to put particular chapters. With very few exceptions, the authors are not concerned to examine single issues, but to explore connections between them. Analysing single issues in depth can lead to clarity, but it can also be misleading, masking the ambiguities, conflicts and contradictions that occur when theory is translated into practice in real-life school communities. Different authors in this book explore how issues cut across one another; they acknowledge conflicts and tensions; they try not to offer simple solutions to complex problems, but provide signposts for identifying where progress is needed and possible, and ideas for how that progress might be promoted.

Many chapters are case studies of particular schools and classrooms. All are written from a personal perspective, providing examples of equal opportunities in context rather than dealing with issues in an abstract or detached way. We have tried to present a wide range of different school contexts — from inner city to rural, from the north to the south of England, from multiracial, multilingual classrooms to monolingual ones. There are accounts of work from different curriculum areas, and of issues that recur throughout the curriculum. Equal opportunities need to be interpreted and understood in context. What is appropriate in one school or classroom may not be in another. Each different context has its own dynamic, its own constraints, according to the people and institutions involved. Issues of power and inequality will be realised in different ways.

Inevitably, there are gaps. We do not have chapters about the effects of anti-Irish racism, or of anti-semitism, which are important issues for many children and teachers.

Situated accounts of equal opportunities initiatives have an immediate practical value. By showing the constraints under which teachers operate, they allow others both to evaluate the work carried out and to consider how similar ideas might work in other contexts — with different groups of children or in different curriculum areas. Such accounts also make visible the inter-relatedness of different aspects of equal opportunities: curriculum content, teaching approach and classroom organisation; individual practice and whole-school policy; the needs of children and parents, teaching and non-teaching staff.

The work documented in this book, therefore, provides a rich resource of practical ideas. But it also raises questions which need to be faced by all those committed to working for equal opportunities in education:

- How far can or should a school change to meet the needs of individual children or groups of children? How does this affect other children in the school?

- If we are trying to offer more choice to all children, how can those children who are not in a position to take advantage of such choices be enabled to do so?
- When do we need to open up access to particular kinds of knowledge, and when call into question the nature of the knowledge on offer?
- How can we respect difference without suggesting that 'anything goes'?
- Some equal opportunities work creates conflict. How do we deal with this?
- If we work to give more power to some children, or parents, or teachers, does this mean taking it away from others?
- How can we practise as well as preach equality, at a whole school level?

Overview of Contents

Part I: Children

Much has been written within the educational literature, about inequalities between different groups of children: inequalities based principally on class, 'race' and gender. Here we have tried to include a broader range of issues, and also to show that schools' responses to different children need to take account of a complex range of factors: social, educational and contextual.

The chapters focusing primarily on children deal with gender, 'race', disability, learning difficulties, language and culture, and class. Elsewhere, there are chapters on bullying and sexuality (see Chapters 15 and 18). However, these issues are not treated as if they were discrete — we have tried to show how, in practice, they often intersect. Diane Reay's chapter on working with boys in an infant classroom shows how gender was a powerful factor in enabling some boys to challenge her authority as a female teacher. However, she also felt she needed to take account of other dimensions — in this case principally 'race' and class — to understand and deal with the boys' behaviour and attitudes towards their work. Beate Schmidt-Rohlfing, in her account of Asian deaf children's education in the mainstream classroom, argues that this is not simply a question of accommodating children with a 'disability': issues of language and culture are also at stake. And in 'Looking back', the secondary school girls who reflect on their experiences of primary education see many connections between 'race' and gender.

Other chapters deal with issues that have not always featured on the equal opportunities agenda. Brian Foster discusses the hostility with which Traveller children are frequently faced, and Andrew Pritchard describes a project that set out to counteract this. Lynda Yard, in her chapter on children who don't stand out, suggests that we need to look beyond conventional social categories: there is a variety of ways in which children can be denied access to the curriculum or to school and classroom life, and a variety of ways in which schools can respond to the needs of different children.

One response to diversity, stressed in several chapters, is that everyone in the school should be involved in creating an equitable working environment. In Beate Schmidt-Rohlfing's school, for instance, many hearing staff and pupils are able to communicate with deaf pupils in British Sign Language. Alyson Clare, in her account of Chris Raine's progress, shows how important it has been for all those involved in a local primary school — pupils, teaching staff, the driver of the school bus — to work together to support a child with Down's Syndrome. Alyson argues convincingly that other pupils, as well as Chris, have benefited from his presence in the school. She also points out that, while schools need to recognise differing abilities and skills, they need at the same time to offer a range of new experiences and challenges to all children.

Providing equal opportunities is not just about recognising and responding to difference, it is also about empowering people — empowering girls relative to boys, black people relative to white people, Travellers relative to settled people. And it is about empowering parents, involving them in decisions about their children's education (there is more on working with parents in Part III). The secondary school girls looking back comment that they wish their teachers had done more to support them in their attempts to resist racism and sexism. Providing this level of support, however, may mean that teachers have to deal with conflicting interests: for instance, Diane Reay expresses her own misgivings about devoting extra time to working with boys, 'an already privileged group'. Teachers concerned to provide equal opportunities necessarily lay themselves open to challenge, and will have to deal with values that may be different from their own. Empowerment is neither an easy nor a comfortable process.

Part II: Classrooms and curriculum

In one way or another, the seven chapters in this part of the book move on debates about the implementation of equal opportunities in primary classrooms. The first three chapters look beneath bland and worthy statements about 'entitlement', and explore some of the necessary conditions for genuine access and empowerment to occur. The authors of 'Story Box', 'Global Education for Equality' and 'Some Equality Issues in Primary Design and Technology' argue that a multicultural approach which celebrates diversity is necessary, but does not go far enough in challenging prejudice and inequality. As Margot Brown points out in 'Global Education', children need education *about* equality, *for* equality and *in* equality.

In these three chapters, power in the classroom and the nature of the curriculum become focal issues. Classroom dynamics are brought centre stage. Child-centred starting points are interpreted to mean that the cultural and linguistic resources of groups of children who are regularly marginalised or disparaged are not just given a token nod, but introduced as the main content of the curriculum. The authors offer strategies to empower children — but more than this: they suggest how the overt curriculum can offer opportunities for developing children's ability to think about equality issues and learn to work in more egalitarian ways. None pretends that such approaches are completely conflict free — for them as teachers or for children learning to take control of their learning.

The chapter on 'Aprons and Attitudes' is rather different in that it is less about classroom practice *per se* and more concerned with asking teachers to think professionally about and critique conventional anti-sexist analyses of children's books. Sue Adler extends to the primary school a long-standing debate between feminists, exploring the tension between concern for 'equal rights', where females may well be encouraged to be like males, and acknowledging and valuing different female interests and talents. Using this analysis, she examines in new and provocative ways a number of children's books which are in regular use in primary classrooms. She invites teachers to reassess how and why they use children's literature to promote equality.

Finally, there are three chapters looking at equal opportunities issues in the assessment of, respectively, mathematics and science, humanities and language. Across these different areas of the curriculum, several common themes emerge: the need to take account of children's diverse experiences; to plan for contexts that will allow children to be assessed 'at their best'; and to counter stereotypes and misperceptions.

Part III: Whole school

'If segregation of the sexes or races prevails, if authoritarianism and hierarchy dominate the system, the child cannot help but learn that power and status are the dominant factors in human relationships. If, on the other hand, the school system is democratic, if the teacher and child are each respected units, the lesson of respect for the person will easily register. As in society at large, the structure of the pedagogical system will blanket, and may negate, the specific intercultural lessons taught.' (Allport, 1954: 511)

'Equal opportunities are not just a matter of good classroom practice, but of school organisation and management.' (Jackie Hughes)

As Allport pointed out nearly 40 years ago, the way children and adults treat each other within a school and the overall approaches of that school to power relationships in teaching and learning will probably have a far more lasting effect on children's attitudes towards justice and equality than individual classroom activities. The authors in this final section look at how to address equal opportunities issues at a whole school level. All five are concerned with the relationship between policy and practice. On the one hand, school structures need to be developed which encourage and support cooperation and equality, and on the other individual members of the school community need actively to reflect on, and contribute to that development on a day to day basis. As Pete Sanders argues, a policy only works if it is lived out in a pattern of ongoing relationships and activities. Pete Sanders and Jackie Hughes are both head teachers. Pete looks at ways of developing a non-hierarchical style of management, where all staff will feel valued, and reflects on the implications of this for his own role as head. Jackie describes how as a new head she tackled the business of moving the school towards more direct consideration of equal opportunities issues both at a practical level and, later, in school policies. Ann Watson has been involved in the development of equal opportunities work in her school over the past ten years, and draws some conclusions from this longer term perspective. She looks in particular at how work with parents has been an integral part of the development of school structures and the school curriculum.

The remaining two chapters focus on the need for whole school work in relation to specific issues. Celestine Keise discusses the widespread and destructive experience of bullying among children, and shows how a planned period of in-service work can have important effects for both staff and pupils. Paul Patrick and Helena Burke tackle one of the most controversial areas of equal opportunities work, attitudes towards sexuality. They argue strongly that an equal opportunities policy cannot work unless it is truly comprehensive. Avoiding one area will undermine the rest, since it will always result in equal opportunities for some, and not for others. They show the importance of a strong policy statement to form the basis for consultation between staff, parents and governors, and how policy, at national and school level, can be used to support and drive practice.

Endeavouring to work in an equal and cooperative way with other adults raises its own dilemmas. Pete Sanders writes about the difficulties of balancing responsibility, delegation and negotiation, and about the consequences of shifts of power within the management structure. Ann Watson, who argues that equal opportunities in school and involvement with parents cannot be separated, points out that if we give more power to others, then we must expect to have to give more weight to, and cope with, their arguments and feelings. In negotiating the difficult path towards more equal and just ways of working together, effective communication is vital. All five authors look at various ways of communicating with and involving other adults across the school.

Consistent and committed equal opportunities work must lead to changes in the overall school ethos. Both Jackie Hughes and Celestine Keise note improvements in terms of discipline and reduction of aggression. Long term positive changes may, as Ann Watson suggests, be more difficult to detect, and we need some kind of evaluation to validate individual impressions and experience.

References

Allport G. W. (1954) *The Nature of Prejudice.* Reading, MA: Addison-Wesley.

National Curriculum Council (NCC) (1989) *English Key Stage 1: Non-Statutory Guidance.* York: NCC.

Statham, J. and Mackinnon, D. with Cathcart, H. and Hales, M. (1991) *The Education Fact File* (2nd edn). London: Hodder and Stoughton in association with The Open University.

Part I:
Children

1 'He Doesn't Like You, Miss': Working with Boys in an Infant Classroom

DIANE REAY

In this chapter Diane Reay reports on her work with a group of disruptive and disaffected boys, who already at the age of six were showing disturbing signs of sexism and alienation from school. She recognises the roles of class and ethnicity as well as gender in understanding children's interactions and behaviour. She is also concerned with the importance of high self esteem, the ability to collaborate and have one's contributions valued. This thought-provoking study points to the value of careful observation of children at work, and sensitivity to children's individual needs. It also offers a strong warning against stereotyping.

Introduction

As an advisory teacher in Equal Opportunities, I have had to respond to a ground-swell of concern about boys' behaviour and achievement. In the last two years over a dozen teachers, all female, have approached me to discuss boys in their class who were presenting problems:

- by demanding an excessively high proportion of teacher time and attention;
- in terms of discipline in both the classroom and the playground;
- through lower levels of engagement with the English curriculum leading to lower levels of achievement than the girls.

This chapter is an account of my attempt to respond to that concern in one classroom, particularly the issues that emerged round class and race as well as gender, and my partial reservations about my intervention and about this focus on boys.

In 1990 I started working as an advisory teacher for Equal Opportunities in Ealing. At initial school-based meetings I discussed the boys' projects I had been involved with in my previous job as a special needs co-ordinator. I seemed to uncover an existing concern, and dealing with boys' behaviour became the main way that I supported the twelve primary schools that I was attached to.

The classroom project described here was in a first school in a leafy, middle-class suburban area. The school has a predominantly white middle-class intake and a reputation for high academic standards. Some teachers spoke of difficulties with a few boys in their class, but the problem seemed to be particularly acute in the Year 2 class (6–7 year olds). This class had had three teachers in the Reception year and there was a gender imbalance of 2:1, with eighteen boys and nine girls. The class was representative of the whole school in that the majority of pupils were white and from middle-class backgrounds and a number of the boys were very motivated, high achievers. However, the class teacher felt that the children had never really settled after their difficult start in school and she was particularly worried about a small group of boys who were messing about rather than working, and preventing other children from learning.

Observation to Establish What the Problem Was

To find out for myself what was going on I made an initial visit and spent an hour and a half observing the whole class. The class were working in five groups, organised by their teacher. For half the time I used a chart to note all the off-task behaviour I could see at five minute intervals. This meant I had ten sets of observations. At first I had thought all the boys' behaviour was uniformly rowdy, but I realised after a while that the majority of the boys were on task most of the time and that their conversation was work related. For example, Jack and Oliver, two white middle-class boys, were on task 10 out of 10 times. Between times — focusing on the boys' behaviour rather than the girls' — I wrote down anything of note, and started to identify that eight boys, spread over the five groups, were responsible for most of the problems, through disruption and being off-task. These were Gary, Osman, Darren, Steven, Peter, Abdul, Tyrone and Mark (in descending order of off-task observations — from 8 out of 10 off-task observations for Gary and Osman to 4 out of 10 for Tyrone and Mark.

For the remaining time I concentrated on what the eight identified boys were doing. Gary threw pencils at a group, composed mainly of girls, who were doing a practical maths activity. There was minimal response; one girl complained to her partner and Gary wandered off and got into a playful fight with another boy. Osman joined in. The teacher intervened, sent

Osman out of the room and gently directed Gary back to the set task. For the next fifteen minutes he sat in front of a blank piece of paper, intermittently making whistling noises. When he was certain the teacher was engrossed in helping another group he slid out of his chair, crawled into the book corner, and furtively started to assemble lego bricks. When a girl came to refer to a book, he yelled at her and kicked out at her leg. Other girls had to suffer more sustained interference. Peter disrupted one girl's learning on four separate occasions. First, he took her pencil from her. She went and found another one. Then he sat down next to her and took away the book she was reviewing. She didn't complain and finished off her review without the book. Twenty minutes later when she was using the computer Peter came across and ran his fingers over the keyboard adding a string of gibberish to her text. Later, he started talking to her about television when she was trying to work on maths.

However, most of the boys' disruptions were directed at each other. There were three fights during the hour and a half that I was there. In addition to the one already mentioned between Gary and Osman, Osman had a fight with Tyrone and there was a scrap between Darren and Abdul. There was also a lot of copycat behaviour. Abdul copied Gary throwing pencils and both Osman and Steven started to make silly noises while Gary was whistling. Most of the girls and Jack and Oliver, seemed to have well rehearsed avoidance strategies when it came to dealing with the 'naughty boys' as some children called them.

As well as helping me find out just what these eight identified boys were doing, close observation helped me understand the dynamics and subtleties of other boys' behaviour. For example, I had initially presumed that Alex, one of the few working-class boys, was working hard. He seemed to be concentrating on his books and for the entire period I was there I did not see him speak to another child. However, far from his energy going into his work it all seemed to be channelled into well developed avoidance strategies. He picked up his pencil, even sharpened it, turned over pages, but never managed to write more than a couple of words. I also discovered that seven boys, and in particular Mark, Tyrone and Abdul had the role of followers, who rarely initiated disruption, but were frequently drawn in by the ring leaders.

Boys who Challenge Female Teachers

As well as disrupting other children, some boys had techniques of challenging female teachers' authority, as this exchange with Steven and Mark reveals. Steven was meticulously illustrating his book review. I praised the drawing, but pointed out that he was supposed to be writing.

Steven ignored me and whispered something to Mark sitting next to him. Mark looked up at me and said 'Steven doesn't like you'. I replied 'That's alright, we can't like everybody'. A few seconds later, I tried again 'Very good, Steven, now it's time to write. Which part of the story did you enjoy the most?'. Steven mumbled inaudibly and reluctantly started to write. A few minutes later, Mark tugged at my sleeve 'Steven doesn't like you at all'. I couldn't resist a moralism, 'Well, I always wait until I know someone a bit better before I make up my mind about them!' Further whispering ensued, then Mark turned to me and delivered Steven's *coup de grace.* 'Steven says you're 35–40, you're a woman, you're a teacher, that's all he needs to know'.

Steven's attempts to put me in my place were not a new experience. As a teacher, both at an off-site unit and in primary classrooms, I have frequently felt oppressed by the boys in my charge. I have been verbally abused and on a number of occasions, physically assaulted. At the time I rationalised that I was not a 'good enough' teacher. Since then I have often seen women teachers in similar situations, challenged and upset by the aggression of a few boys in their class, and realised the problem is not of individual ineptitude, but of sexism. Boys also challenge male teachers, and sometimes draw on gender stereotypes by implying the teacher is not 'a real man'. However disruptive boys seldom rely to the same extent on devaluing male teachers because of their sex.

Steven's resistance to female authority was relatively covert compared to Gary's and Osman's. They did not even pretend to attempt reading or writing tasks but played the clown — throwing pencils, falling off chairs or making silly noises.

Working with a Group of Boys on Making Books

I decided to try and tackle the boys' attitudes to work and to others in the class head on through a group project on bookmaking. After discussion with the class teacher I decided to work with Gary, Osman, Peter, Darren and Alex — who were not only disruptive, but gave the most cause for concern academically. I also included the two very industrious high achievers — Jack and Oliver. Abdul, who was one of the original eight whom I had observed, and Tony (who was not) asked to be included. They were boys who tended to get drawn into copycat behaviour, but most of the time they were conscientious and capable and along with myself, Jack and Oliver, I was confident they would contribute to a small group, with plenty of teacher support.

My goals were relatively modest — to raise the boys' awareness of other children's needs; to increase on-task behaviour; and to support the boys in working collaboratively.

A dismissive comment from Gary in the book corner was our starting point. I asked him to pick up a book he was standing on. 'So what', he had said, 'that's just a girl's book'. I made the problem very general — they were to produce books that both girls and boys would enjoy reading. In our first session we discussed reading preferences, starting with their own, but moving on to think about other children's preferences.

In a study for the ILEA, Pip Osmont found that boys often choose as favourites books that are considered unsuitable for school, for example, 'superman type books', TV books and comics. The preferences of the boys in my group were similar. The highest number of votes went to fantasy books, closely followed by humorous books. They thought that the other boys in the class would have similar tastes, but without prompting suggested that girls' reading preferences were often different. Osman stated that girls liked books with female characters and Jack agreed. I asked how we might check out their ideas; they suggested a whole class survey and set about devising an appropriate questionnaire. The survey was useful as they had to accept that other children, notably girls, had very different preferences, and that these preferences affected what they did next. Initially, the chief difference seemed that the boys were much more interested in non fiction than girls (with sport as their top category). Though fantasy was just as popular with girls as with boys, a follow-up survey revealed that the boys voted overwhelmingly for books about heroes, while the girls preferred fairy stories and books about magic.

Next the group had to produce proposals for books that appealed to the widest possible readership in the class, finding ways to accommodate the girls' preferences as well as their own. I had expected dissent. There was none. Instead there was a real effort to comply, influenced by Jack and Oliver's contagious enthusiasm. Though the storyline for one book was extremely stereotyped, with Michael Jackson kidnapping Kylie Minogue, who is rescued by Jason Donovan, the two boys responsible rationalised that girls enjoyed reading anything about Kylie Minogue while boys would enjoy the adventure. Nearly all the other boys managed to reconcile their own interests with those of their classmates. For example, Darren and Abdul wrote a fantasy adventure story about a monkey called Mitur, who has magical powers. Mitur sets out on a journey and on the way meets four different people — a young boy, a female teacher, an old woman and a poor man — who all need help in solving difficult problems. Abdul and Darren tried very hard to meet the set objectives and were the only two in the group to check with some of the girls whether their storyline was popular. The rest just canvassed other members of the group.

To my surprise Jack and Oliver had most difficulty catering for the girls' interests. Their book was about a plane crashing in the desert, leaving two boys orphaned and stranded with only five days provisions. They were enormously enthusiastic, but their confidence and sense of knowing best meant they were the least open to suggestions from me and other members of the group.

In a small group setting the five boys who regularly used avoidance strategies of either disruption or withdrawal were much easier to motivate. Like the rest of the group, they enjoyed being consulted on the content and the process of the task, and responded well to clear instructions and concise boundaries around behaviour.

'Therapeutic' Effects of the Project for Some of the Boys

There was an interesting and unexpected outcome from the bookmaking project for three of the boys who experienced the most difficulty in the classroom. Gary, Osman and Alex were still emergent readers, who baulked at any writing task. So I suggested they use a book which was a favourite with both boys and girls as a basis for their own story and offered to scribe for them. Osman and Gary chose *Angry Arthur* as a model and collaborated on a book about feelings, with themselves as the central characters. Their two male protagonists swung from destructive rage through catharsis to relief and happiness and offered some interesting insights into what may be going on for them (see the page from *Grumpy Gary and Sad Osman* reproduced opposite). In the original, *Angry Arthur*, the main character is extremely powerful and wreaks havoc all around him. In contrast Gary and Osman's characters are helpless victims of an external havoc over which they have no control. In the end everybody agrees to tidy up and the main characters feel much more positive about themselves. Already at the age of six, most of Gary and Osman's feelings of self-worth seemed to come from presenting themselves as 'tough' and 'cool' — and investing in a male persona which largely precluded academic success. The male role models in this class were middle class and high achieving and from my amateur reading of the text I wondered how far these two — unlike most of the other boys in the class — were experiencing tension and conflict because these role models seemed unattractive and probably out of reach.

Alex chose a book called *My Friend Does Not Live Here Any More*. He changed the main protagonist from male to female and then wrote his own version about a child who began the story lonely and friendless and ended it with a new found friend. He was the only child who was unable to work

Everywhere that Gary went a giant mess followed him around. It made him sad
and it made him angry. He wanted the world to be a tidy place.

collaboratively which backed up my initial observations that he communicated with nobody.

Conclusions: The Influence and Interaction of Class, 'Race' and Gender

In a small group, without responsibility for the whole class, I could
realise my goals. The class teacher, who was an excellent primary practitioner, was not so fortunate. She had inherited a class where the ratio of
boys to girls was two to one, and where a number of boys had succeeded
in creating an ethos which was anti-authority and anti-work. Perhaps the
inconsistency in their early schooling was responsible. However, I think
the situation bears deeper analysis. In trying to account for learning difficulties one can look to the characteristics of individual children, their
motivation and attitude, ability and confidence and take no account of
broader issues. However these aspects of educational progress and achievement are themselves often connected with class, gender and 'race'. With
respect to class, I am sure it is significant that while most of the children in
the class and indeed in the school, were middle-class, four out of five of the
boys causing greatest concern about behaviour and difficulties with literacy
were working-class (Gary, Osman, Darren and Alex). Of all the children in
the class, these four had most difficulty with tasks set by their teacher and
with peer-group relations. 'Race' also needs to be considered. Both Osman
and Abdul came from ethnic minority backgrounds whereas the majority
of the children in the class were white. Peter Woods (1990) has suggested

that where ethnic minority children are heavily outnumbered they may experience feelings of ostracism and alienation.

My work in the class did not allow me to do more than speculate about these two aspects of their difficulties, but I do feel I can speak with more confidence about gender. It is not new for primary schools to wrestle with boys' underachievement in reading and writing. In this class the problem had become highly visible. Osman, Gary, Alex and Darren all had obvious difficulties with literacy, compounded by lack of motivation, lack of confidence and I would suggest, their own perceptions of appropriate male behaviour. It is unwise to generalise from a handful of cases and even here there seem to be different reasons for the boys' alienation. Darren seemed more a follower than a leader of disruption when his behaviour was closely observed. Alex's poignant contribution in the project hints at difficulties which were not just to do with allying himself with a macho anti-authority peergroup. However, Gary and Osman seemed hardly to identify with the values of their female middle-class teachers, even in infant school; these boys seemed to regard reading and writing as 'feminine' occupations, inconsistent with their male self-image.

There is research evidence that when academic success is difficult to achieve, and possibilities of excelling in other contexts are limited, children regularly turn to disruption to gain attention and recognition. Osman, Gary and Darren seemed to feel entitled to centrality as males and sought status in resistance and challenge to authority. I believe that they succeeded in building up a power base for a number of reasons starting with the gender imbalance in the class and because they managed to draw into their sphere of influence a further group of boys. Tyrone, Mark and Abdul all fell victim to Gary and Osman's macho culture and, although quite unmacho themselves, felt pressurised to conform.

However, by the end of the year the teacher's persistence and good practice had succeeded in manoeuvring most of the boys out of the orbit of the ringleaders. She invested a great deal of time and energy in ensuring that boys on the periphery of the disruption, such as Tyrone, Mark and Abdul — followers rather than leaders — saw their best interests in following *her* lead instead. She was also successful in drawing Darren away from Gary and Osman's influence. She spent a lot a time with the whole class establishing positive but concise rules about behaviour and clear procedures for carrying out tasks. She set up systems of rewards and sanctions; she negotiated curriculum content and work quotas with the children. The atmosphere in the classroom became increasingly work orientated.

However, Gary and Osman still spent far more time off than on task. Their success in the book-making project had depended on teacher attention which was not feasible at a whole class level. In a schooling system which prioritises academic achievement the losers will be children like Gary and Osman, who resist the imposition of academic values and frequently opt out of learning. Increasingly my work as a primary practitioner has caught me up in the struggles of such boys, leaving me with unanswered questions about the relationship of gender, 'race' and class and how far I should be devoting my energy to boys, who already demand disproportionate amounts of teacher time and attention, at the expense of girls.

Reference

Osmont, P. (1987) *Stop, Look and Listen*. London: ILEA.
Woods, P. (1990) *The Happiest Days? How Pupils Cope With School*. London: Falmer Press.

2 Chris Raine's Progress[1]

ALYSON CLARE

Chris Raine is a child with Down's Syndrome who attends a small village school in Cumbria. Alyson Clare's chapter describes his school life in some detail, but also raises wider issues: how can schools respond effectively to diversity amongst their pupils? How can they both recognise difference (and not expect children to conform to unreasonable demands), and also ensure all children are challenged and encouraged to participate in a wide range of activities? Alyson shows how much Chris has benefited from attending his local school; she also argues convincingly that other pupils have benefited socially and academically from Chris' presence.

Introduction and Background

In September 1987 we at Ravenstonedale School admitted seven reception children. One of them, Chris Raine, had Down's Syndrome. This is the story of Chris' time at Ravenstonedale School. It is a personal and individual story, but it also raises equal opportunities issues that are relevant to other children, and other contexts.

Despite the wishes of his parents, the recommendations of various people who had monitored Chris' development since birth and our willingness to try to integrate and educate him at Ravenstonedale, the authority had originally decided to send Chris to Sandgate School in Kendal, over 20 miles from his home. Everyone concerned appealed against this decision and eventually it was decided that Chris should be educated within a day special school or special education unit. However Chris should initially be admitted to the local primary school with individual support. He should transfer to a special school at a later date. We admitted Chris and with him came Rana Coleman our newly appointed Special Attachment Welfare Assistant (SAWA).

Julia Holloway the infant teacher and I spent a great deal of time discussing and planning for the day Chris started school. I had had a little experience working with children with disabilities but Julia had had none and although very willing to try, was initially and quite understandably, apprehensive. We had many positive things on our side, not the least of which were parental and community support. Ravenstonedale and Newbiggin-on-Lune (the village one mile away where Chris lives) are very rural. Consequently everyone knows everyone else. Mr and Mrs Raine had purposely strived to make Chris a part of this community from an early age. He had attended chapel and the parent-run playgroup regularly. All 33 children at school knew Chris and, having talked to them, we anticipated that they would be protective towards Chris and make allowances for the fact that he was different.

Another positive factor was the SAWA. Initially the authority had offered us help for 15 hours per week but Chris was still in nappies and we did not think him capable of restricting his need for clean nappies to coincide with the 15 hours a SAWA would be present! Rana was consequently appointed full-time for 30 hours per week.

The local speech therapist, physiotherapist and pre-school teacher for children with learning difficulties would all be available to help us on what felt like a journey into the unknown. Even the school bus drivers were willing to take care of Chris on the school bus, enabling him to be as much like the other children as possible. It seemed like a very tall order at the outset, but our philosophy was that if Chris was to be educated at Ravenstonedale, he was to be treated as much like the other children as we could. If concessions were to be made they must be for a specific purpose and for as short a time as possible. We would, of course, have back-up from the educational psychologist and from the experienced staff at Sandgate Special School.

So, with all this ready to support us, Chris started school. With him he brought his dinner money, his PE bag and just four distinguishable words — 'mummy', 'daddy', 'car', 'bus' and within a week, a fifth one, 'school'.

Early Language Development

Initially, our primary concern was to get Chris settled into school. For the first two sessions Mrs Raine stayed with him. It was clear from the start that there would not be a problem integrating Chris socially. He joined in classroom activities quite happily and ran to children he knew in the playground; they were only too pleased to play with him. We wondered what would happen when the 'honeymoon' period was over but the children settled into what we consider to be a healthy, caring, no-fuss relationship with Chris. They will play with him and give him the extra time he needs to take part but they are also fair and firm and do not make too many concessions or allow unacceptable behaviour.

One of the oldest girls, Nicki, became a firm favourite with Chris. She spent a great deal of time during playtimes and before school playing with him, talking to him, encouraging him and teaching him new skills. The period before school started had been a worry to us. The school bus would arrive over 20 minutes before school started, at which time Rana would arrive. The children had always been encouraged to use this time constructively with toys, sand, drawing, writing, reading etc. Chris fell into this pattern quite easily. It was useful to us for two reasons; firstly, we became aware of Chris' quite extraordinary powers of concentration when looking at books; secondly, it became obvious just how much he could learn from other children and how much they could learn from him.

Nicki and some other children spent the first few weeks teaching Chris to draw faces. He was keen to please and to copy what the others were doing. The one big problem Chris encountered was real communication with the rest of us. The pre-school teacher for children with learning difficulties, Mrs Tipping, and her replacement, Maureen Ellis, had told us that Chris' understanding of language far outstripped his spoken language. We found that Chris could follow even quite complicated instructions easily, especially if you made certain you had his full attention in the first place. Situations arose, however, where Chris could not make himself understood. We would try various suggestions but if they were wrong Chris would become frustrated or even resign himself to the fact that he could not make us understand. On reflection, the children coped better with this situation than we did. Perhaps they did not expect to be able to meet all his needs or wants. They would simply distract him and do something else with him. As adults, we found the situation upsetting, frustrating and unacceptable.

The speech therapists, Pauline Smithson and Tara Winterton, offered a possible solution; they would teach us, along with Chris, to use Makaton sign language[2]. Initially, we did not really see Makaton as a solution, more as a means of attacking the problem. We were worried that Chris would come to rely on Makaton at the expense of developing speech. Julia, Rana and I discussed the matter and felt it was worth trying, so we approached Mrs Raine. If this were really to be beneficial to Chris, she would have to learn it too — and so, we decided, would all the other children in school.

Pauline agreed to come to school about once a week, for about twenty minutes, to teach us all in stages. The adults admitted to feeling a little nervous about learning this new skill. The children took to it like ducks to water, including Chris! From the youngest infants to the oldest juniors the children picked up the signs very easily, often recalling them more readily than the adults. After four or five sessions and lots of practice we had all mastered the first four stages. This enabled us to sign many of the words one would need in simple conversation with a four or five-year-old. Signs like 'egg', 'biscuit' and 'jam' were not so important for us in school but 'play', 'ball', 'book' and 'crayon' were. Throughout the learning period, Pauline repeatedly stressed that we must always say the words as we used the signs. Makaton was not only to help Chris to communicate, it was to encourage him to speak too.

We still recall with pleasure the times when Chris used a new sign spontaneously for the first time. He could now sign 'ball' and one of the children would get him one. But this did not last for long. The children began to demand 'ball please' of him and Chris obliged. And then it was 'play ball please'... We had a slight worry that parents might object to their children learning Makaton but we had some very positive feedback and know that more than a few parents learned a new skill from their children during those weeks!

Then spoken language began to appear with the signs, slowly and sometimes indistinctly at first, often in a whisper until he gained in confidence. We knew Chris had difficulty in making some sounds but he could make reasonable approximations. We, staff and children, were quite firm at this stage about encouraging Chris to verbalise as well as sign. To encourage him to speak out and not just whisper, Pauline brought us a new gadget. It was a large, red plastic apple. If Chris held it close to his mouth and said a word loudly, a worm would pop out of the top of the apple. Whisper a word and the worm would not appear. This helped a great deal. Like all five-year-olds, there were times when he would try to get away with as little effort as possible but on the whole he was co-operative and keen to imitate the others.

By the time Christmas came around we were all in full flow with Makaton. It seemed to the children a natural progression to incorporate it into our Christmas production. We were performing a Nativity Play with the infants acting, the juniors reading from the Bible, and everyone singing. It wasn't long before the infants were signing as they acted so we wrote them a very simple script which was a compromise between the Authorised Version and the range of Makaton signs they knew. Chris was a shepherd boy and with a few others had to say 'Where's the Baby?' and 'Let's go to see the baby'. Despite the fact that he wouldn't wear his head-dress, he was excellent at the dress rehearsal. In the actual performance he was too tired and simply lay down. Nevertheless, we were very proud of him.

One set of signs we all learned was the set for letter names. The infants learned them as the sounds the letters make and developed a little game with them. When it was time to go somewhere — to dinner, to the playground or to put coats on — one child would say, 'If your name begins with 'a' you can go'. At the same time they would make the sign. Chris loved to be the one in control and very soon could look at each child quite pointedly and make the sign for the sound their name began with, thereby allowing them to go. For this game, Chris did not verbalise the sounds, we encouraged him to say the child's name. Some of them, especially the long ones, were very indistinct at first. Many sounds were difficult for him, thus 'Laura' sounded more like 'oors'. We encouraged him to say the longer names syllabically so that 'Al' eventually grew to be Alexander. Each time we had to make sure that Chris was watching our mouths and trying to copy. Occasionally this syllabic method back-fired; Chris now calls James, Jamers with two very distinct syllables. No-one seems to mind.

In one-to-one situations with Rana, Chris was now being encouraged to use two words together, e.g. 'pink pig' or 'black cat'. His one-to-one correspondence was very good and his number words quite distinct so 'three dogs' or 'ten apples' were fairly distinguishable and within his capabilities. Chris was quite happy to repeat these phrases after somebody else. However, with a picture of two pink pigs before him, Chris would only say 'pigs'. He was unable to use more than one word spontaneously, with the exception of the phrase 'play ball'.

It is, perhaps, appropriate to mention here some of Chris' other achievements apart from in the area of oral language development. His gross motor control and general co-ordination were vastly improved; he was well-adjusted socially; he could trace or draw recognisable pictures; he could copy-write and write his name unaided; he had learned to take his turn; he had begun a toilet-training programme and was making slow but steady progress; and he was happy.

Further Initiatives

Chris' lack of spontaneous oral language to communicate with the rest of us was the next obstacle to be overcome. We knew he could say strings of words but we were unsure how meaningful they were to him. We needed to devise further strategies to develop this aspect of his language. Our close monitoring of his development to date meant we knew exactly where he was at. Two possible lines of attack seemed open to us: these were his obvious love of books and his ability with numbers. Add to this his strong desire to do what the others could do, and we had the beginnings of a new programme of work for Chris.

The overall plan was to saturate Chris with language. He needed to hear lots of meaningful sentences spoken directly to him and to be encouraged to repeat phrases and sentences in a specific context. Apart from doing this through games, speech therapy exercises, normal conversation etc., the main areas of attack were to be through the reading scheme (Ginn 360), other books, and the maths scheme (Peak). As his drawing improved and became more recognisable another line of attack was to get him to write sentences with his picture and read them to anyone with the time to listen!

Chris' love of books is quite remarkable for a child of his age. It is not unusual for him to look at books on his own for more than 20 minutes. He often takes a book to Rana to read to him. His visual memory is excellent but it still surprised us all when he began to assimilate the sight vocabulary for Level One of the reading scheme. In some of the books the sentences are actually questions requiring a one word answer. When Chris answered these spontaneously it indicated to us that he understood at least some of the strings of words he was verbalising. Rana asked Mrs Raine for some photographs of Chris when he was younger and made a book out of them with spaces for Chris to write about himself. Chris had already learned the word 'me', but the book was useful to reinforce this and to encourage the use of 'I' and 'mine'. It also encouraged him to talk about events in the past, something he had found difficult. He also enjoyed acting out events so Rana could guess what he was doing.

Evaluation: January 1989

It is now 17 months since Chris started at Ravenstonedale School. Occasionally when we find it difficult to understand something Chris is desperate to communicate to us we recall the early days when this happened many times a day. It is a much rarer occurrence now and that in itself means we have made progress. But how much? What has happened to the Makaton? Have we been able to achieve our aim of getting Chris to communicate in sentences? Chris' expressive language is now largely limited to three or four word phrases but the elements of a sentence, subject-verb-object, are often there. He communicates spontaneously with adults and other children far more frequently and he can expand on what he has said more readily now when prompted. The speech therapist tells us that 'flaccid oral musculature' contributes to his difficulty in articulating certain sounds and we are working on exercises to improve this.

Two weeks ago, just after the school bus arrived, I heard someone crying in the cloakroom. It was Chris; two top-infant girls were trying to find out what was wrong. They said they thought he wanted to play with the football he had brought to school that morning. Chris is difficult to understand when he is crying so I aimed for some one word responses. The conversation went like this:

Me: Did you bring a ball to school this morning, Chris?
Chris: Yes.

Me: Do you want to play with it?

Chris: Yes.

At this point I wasn't going to let him get away with two one word answers so I asked, 'Where do you want to play with it?' hoping for 'In the playground' but the response came after a very deep breath and it was: 'Please I play Chris' ball?' The girls were so excited they rushed off to tell Mrs Holloway.

Over 17 months, our achievements with Chris, or perhaps we should say Chris' own achievements, have been remarkable. Makaton became a thing of the past months ago. One tiny vestige of it remains ... Chris still uses the sign for thank you. On most occasions Chris can make himself understood using words and gestures though it is easier to follow what he says in context rather than out of context. It is getting easier all the time but sometimes we seem to make little progress. 'Hasten slowly' is perhaps a good motto to bear in mind. Chris is contributing to his class and is, in turn, benefiting from the contact with his peers. Just like any other child, Chris can be demanding, exasperating and frustrating but he has added a new dimension to the lives of everyone at Ravenstonedale School and it is a joy to have him with us.

Some Equality Issues

Like any child, Chris had to face many new challenges when he started school. But the onus was also on us to work out how to respond to Chris' needs. We had to make adaptations within the school, rather than expecting Chris simply to fit in with our existing practice. Sometimes, this involved extra resources — we relied on support from Rana, and we needed advice from other professionals. But it was important that all those associated with the school — teachers, children, the drivers of the school bus — worked together to make Ravenstonedale a welcoming place for Chris.

As a school, we needed to recognise the respects in which Chris was different from other children (whilst also recognising that children are quite diverse anyway). But we also had to learn not to make too many concessions. It is important that Chris, like other children, is challenged and stretched, and that he is able to take part in all aspects of school life.

Chris has clearly learned a lot from working with other children, but they, too, have benefited from the experience. They have undoubtedly developed more positive attitudes towards disability and difference, but they have also benefited academically: explaining something to another child is an excellent aid to learning; and in helping Chris' language development, and using

Makaton themselves, the children have gained invaluable insights about language.

I mentioned earlier that we were lucky in having a supportive community — and in that Chris was well-liked and mixed easily with other children. Different strategies might be needed in a large urban school, or for a child who settled in less easily. But schools should be adaptable enough to cope with children with diverse needs — to the benefit of individual children and the schools themselves.

Update: January 1991

Chris has now been at Ravenstonedale School for nearly three and a half years and he continues to make steady progress. There have been three intakes of four-year-olds whilst Chris has been with us and they have easily fallen into the general air of acceptance of Chris' differences. Socially Chris gravitates towards younger children who are engaged in activities more appropriate to him. Now he is a year 3 child, officially a 'junior', he spends part of each day in the junior classroom. He could probably cope in a class of Year 3 children but a village school class of Year 3 to Year 6 children cannot offer all the play activities Chris still needs.

Chris' oral language continues to improve and one aim at the moment is to encourage the use of more complex sentences of six words or more. Another is to use, where appropriate, 'I' and 'my' instead of 'Chris'.

After an absence of more than six months I returned to school recently and was staggered by the improvement in the clarity of his speech. His willingness to contribute comments to the discussion of a story was also notable.

There is still a long road ahead and we are unsure how long Chris will be able to remain at our school with support. Until we hear differently we will continue to be proud of all his achievements and to feel privileged to have been witness to them.

Acknowledgement

Credit for Chris' development to date must be given to his class teacher, Mrs Julia Holloway, the SAWA, Mrs Rana Coleman, the support services, the children at his school and his parents who have supported all our efforts with Chris.

Notes

1. An earlier version of this chapter appeared originally in Booth *et al.* (1992).

2. Makaton is a vocabulary of signs taken from British Sign Language. It is not a complete language (for instance, it doesn't have a grammar). It is often used with people identified as having severe learning difficulties.

References

Booth, T. Swann, W., Masterton, M. and Potts, P. (eds) (1992) *Learning for All, 1: Curriculum for Diversity in Education.* London: Routledge.

3 Signing in Class

BEATE SCHMIDT-ROHLFING

This chapter, like the previous one, is about how schools can support diversity. Beate Schmidt-Rohlfing tells the story of Amad, a young deaf child attending a primary school where he is taught alongside other deaf and hearing pupils. Deafness is seen as a cultural issue rather than simply as a disability: in school, British Sign Language is the main language of teaching and learning for deaf children, although the children also learn English. British Sign Language also provides access to the Deaf community and to Deaf culture. However, the eight deaf children who attend Beate's school come from Punjabi-speaking homes. Beate describes how the school attempts to deal with highly complex linguistic and cultural issues. At the end of the chapter a brief note provides background information on the education of deaf children.

Introduction

The following terms are used in this chapter:

- *British Sign Language* (BSL) is the language of the deaf community in Britain. It is a visual/gestural language. Whereas spoken English uses a combination of sounds to produce words, BSL uses a combination of handshapes, hand positions and movements, body positions and facial expressions to produce signs. BSL has its own distinct grammar. This is not the same as the grammar of English.
- *Sign Supported English* (SSE) is the use of spoken English, with English word order but accompanied by signing. Normally only key-words are signed since it is not possible to speak English and use BSL completely simultaneously.
- *Total communication* is a philosophy in the education of deaf and hearing impaired children. It encourages the use of whatever communication method is most appropriate for the needs of the child. This may include spoken English (with lip reading or amplification of residual hearing); written English; English with sign support; and BSL.

I am a teacher of the deaf in 'Bromleigh'[1] first school in Leeds. I work as part of a team supporting eight deaf children who, since 1987, have been integrated into mainstream schools. If you walk into my classroom you might see groups of children busily discussing their work, much as in any primary classroom. At the corner of one table, discussion is marked by a series of rapid hand movements: two children and a teacher 'talk' silently in British Sign Language (BSL). Leeds integration policy has been designed to provide equal opportunities for deaf children — the opportunity to be educated alongside their hearing peers and, perhaps more fundamentally, the opportunity to use BSL as a language of education and everyday communication in school. I shall describe this policy briefly, then show how it works by focusing on the experiences of one pupil, whom I shall call Amad, and who attends Bromleigh School.

A Policy Framework

Until 1987, partially-hearing children in Leeds (depending on their degree of deafness and their general level of ability) were integrated individually with regular supervision from a peripatetic teacher of the deaf, or educated in one of two partially hearing units. All other deaf and hearing impaired children were educated at the school for the deaf. In September 1987 several primary, middle and high schools in Leeds became 'resourced' to cater for groups of hearing impaired and deaf children, and the school for the deaf closed.

This change in provision was accompanied by other policy changes. At the deaf school all children had been educated orally. Now, Leeds adopted the philosophy of Total Communication: deaf children were entitled to an education using a variety of communication methods, including BSL. The newly appointed Head of the Hearing Impaired Service in Leeds was responsible for implementing this policy, but it is significant that pressure for change came from the deaf community in Leeds, who argued that deaf children should have BSL as their first language, with English taught as a second/foreign language. To support the new policy, Leeds Education Authority employed deaf adults, trained as 'Deaf Instructors' to work alongside teachers of the deaf in the resourced primary schools. Deaf Instructors have BSL as their first language and thus are able to teach deaf children in BSL, while the teacher of the deaf continues to be responsible for teaching English, written and orally as appropriate and giving access to other areas of the curriculum. The policy is premised on the belief that deaf children must have access to their own language, BSL, especially those deaf children for whom it is the language most readily acquired, the preferred means of expression and the basis of cognitive growth. But they are also entitled to learn to speak English, and the teacher of the deaf provides opportunities for this.

The situation in Bromleigh school is, however, more complex: 75% of the children attending the school are of Asian origin, and most have Punjabi as their home language. The eight deaf children at Bromleigh all come from Punjabi-speaking homes. There are, therefore, three languages at issue: BSL, Punjabi and English. Some Asian deaf children understand some Punjabi spoken in the home (using lip reading). Others are not able to do this. At school, BSL is the main language of teaching and learning, and we have also been able to introduce written and spoken English. Punjabi is used in communication with parents, but we have not yet been able to offer formal support to deaf children's home language in school. This is an issue I return to below.

Amad's Day

Amad is a seven-year-old prelingually-deaf Asian boy, the oldest child in his family. The language spoken in Amad's home is Punjabi but he communicates with his mother through gesture, mime and some BSL. I know from our school's home-school liaison teacher that Amad, like some other deaf children, has behaviour problems at home related to difficulties in communication. Amad began at Bromleigh school in 1988. He uses two languages in school, BSL and English. In spring 1991 he was able to use BSL during the first trial run of the SATs.

I have sketched out below a typical timetable for Amad.

9–9.30: Assembly: Amad attends 'Good Work' assembly (in which children display and talk about their work) and Birthday assembly regularly. In addition he attends any special occasion assembly like an Eid assembly. He may also spend this time in an individual session with me, or with Judith Collins, the Deaf Instructor who works with him.

9.30–10.25: This period is usually used for specific language work, signed, written and oral and introduced through BSL by Judith. The session may take place in the 'base' (a room specially equipped for meeting the needs of deaf children) or in the mainstream classroom where some hearing children may join in the same activity.

10.50–12.00: During this session Amad has access to the mainstream curriculum for subjects other than English. I may act as an interpreter in this session.

1.05–2.25: A variety of things take place during the first afternoon session. It may be used for trips to provide interesting first hand experiences for the deaf children. Once a week the children go to an all deaf playgroup (run by Deaf Instructors) where they meet deaf peers from other resourced schools. Alternatively, they may join PE or games lessons or continue with work left from the morning.

2.25–2.45: This session is usually reserved for a story in BSL told by Judith. One of the children may act out or retell the story. The children often play games to help BSL skills. Sometimes the session is used to introduce stories in English (via Sign Supported English), or to read well-known stories in English without signing to encourage speaking.

Assemblies

I often attend 'good work' assemblies with Amad and other deaf children to act as interpreter. Amad enjoys this individual attention, but he is not really interested in any other good work but his own. Instead of watching me and looking at the work presented he tries to use this period to discuss other issues, for example 'Are we going to the University playgroup this afternoon?'. I remind him that he is expected to behave the same as the other children during assembly time, and thus is not allowed to 'talk'. When he is called out to show his piece of good work, I interpret between him and the teacher in charge of the assembly, but their conversation tends to be rather more brief than those between hearing children and the teacher. Both the teacher and Amad need to get more used to communicating through an interpreter. But Amad gets his 'good work sticker' the same as the other children and is very proud. During Birthday assembly Amad finds it harder still to pay attention. He sits with two other deaf peers and the temptation to 'talk' silently is often too great. He joins in some of the songs that are interpreted, but only sporadically. Assemblies are a good opportunity for Amad to get used to an interpreter, a skill he will need throughout his life.

Specific language work

The majority of specific language work is conducted through an approach called DART (Directed Activities Related to Text). Our school is committed to this approach which targets specific English language skills very precisely and thus benefits second language learners. The DART approach leaves scope to target the needs of different children very accurately, while everybody in the class works on the same topic. Amad enjoys these sessions as long as he doesn't have to do any drawings, which he dislikes. He is usually quick to understand the task and works well independently.

Work in the mainstream classroom

In the mainstream classroom Amad likes playing in the office and shop. He loves to hold the gadgets that go with each place and occasionally gets into conflict with another child for holding on to rather than playing with things. He always aims to finish his work quickly so that he can choose what to do next. He is friendly with hearing children on the whole but does not make much effort to communicate with them. He prefers conversing with his two deaf friends, or with Judith or me if he is out of favour with his friends.

If Judith is available, she will work closely with one child while I support a mixed group of deaf and hearing children. Judith provides an adult deaf role model for the deaf as well as the hearing children. Meanwhile, I focus on some aspect of spoken English, and also try generally to aid communication between deaf and hearing children. This need not just involve deaf children using English; hearing children are also keen to communicate in sign. In a recent session Amad and two other deaf children were working on classifying objects. Ruksana, a hearing child, wanted to join the activity but wasn't sure how to begin. I told her to ask Amad, who obviously understood the task. Ruksana asked me for some signs to use — then felt sufficiently confident to try these out with Amad, who responded appropriately. After a few questions, Ruksana understood the activity and was able to join the group.

Lunchtime

I sometimes join the deaf children for lunch, or in the playground. The children tend to sit or play together, but having an interpreter around makes it easier for them to talk with other hearing children. Once Amad told me he did not have chips at home (while sitting in front of his plate of 'school chips'). I repeated his remark orally, as well as signed, and a hearing child joined in the conversation: 'No, we don't either, we have roti'. I repeated this in sign, adding that I liked roti very much myself. Amad then wanted to tell me — and others — how he used roti as a spoon at home to eat dhal. The hearing child had no problem understanding this — it was an experience they had in common and the signs were very descriptive. Both children continued sharing home experiences, using me as an interpreter.

Afternoons

The most exciting afternoon for Amad, no doubt, is Thursday afternoon when he goes to the deaf playgroup run by Deaf Instructors. Here he meets friends from the other resourced schools who all attend this session. The deaf playgroup provides a stress-free environment for Amad: he knows that here he will not miss out on anything and can feel safe and relaxed while also extending his BSL skills.

Friday afternoon is earmarked for doing short trips to give the deaf children first hand experiences they can talk about in BSL to their Deaf Instructor. Follow up work is in English. One Friday we visited a primary school in Bradford with which I had established a link. The school's intake was similar to our own, but it did not cater for deaf children. Children in the reception class were doing a topic on 'My school and friends', the same topic we were covering in Amad's class. The deaf children were fascinated by a different school and classroom, and did not feel threatened by a larger group of hearing children as they were two years younger. The hearing children had learnt some signs and were able to use gesture and mime effectively. Amad had brought a game he had made with his friends and a small group came together to try it out. The children wrote to one another after the visit — mainly in English, but sometimes using Urdu script, and including detailed drawings. We are now planning a return visit.

Amad loves books and always enjoys the story session held during the last half hour of the day. He pays attention when Judith tells the story and actively participates whenever allowed to. He is also happy to be the storyteller himself and would love to be videoed signing a story.

Recently I started experimenting introducing new stories through English/Sign Supported English. They are stories with little text but with

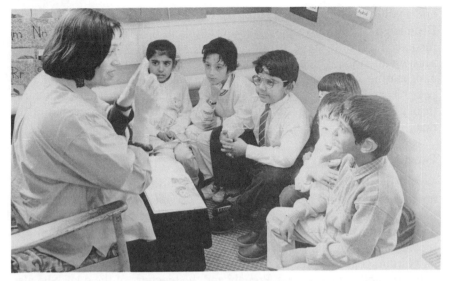

descriptive pictures, and Amad copes easily. He enjoys matching some of the words to pictures and will also try hard to pronounce the words.

Supporting Deaf Bilingual Pupils in the Mainstream School

In order to meet the needs of deaf pupils, schools need external support (in the form of a supportive policy, and additional resources). They also have to be willing to change their own policy and practice. Some of the issues we have had to consider in Bromleigh School, and the changes we have made, or intend making to our policy and practice are set out below.

Adaptations within the school

Schools need some extra funding in order to provide special equipment and additional qualified staff: for instance, Bromleigh has a 'base' room for hearing impaired children, sound-proofed and carpeted and with extra locking up facilities for expensive equipment (radio hearing aids etc.). Some bases also have a flashing light attached to the school bell, a feature which will continue to play an important role in a deaf child's life. The school has two teachers of the deaf and a Deaf Instructor, employed by the Hearing Impaired Service. Older children in secondary school have access to Educational Interpreters and support teachers of the deaf.

But it isn't just a question of providing specialist support. All staff and hearing pupils need preparation to help them accommodate deaf children in the classroom, and around the school. Preparation for staff has included 'Deaf Awareness' sessions, conducted by deaf and hearing professionals, and a voluntary weekly sign language course. Four members of staff from Bromleigh School have gone on to evening sign language classes. Some resourced schools have offered hearing children voluntary lunchtime sessions in BSL, which have helped establish relationships between deaf and hearing children, certainly at primary level. This has not yet been possible at Bromleigh and hearing children learn sign language mainly through mixing with deaf children, and with the aid of the teacher of the deaf.

Parental involvement

At Bromleigh School parents of the deaf children meet for a couple of hours every Friday. They are collected and driven home again, and a creche is provided for young children. Usually the parent support group is well attended and includes parents whose children have left Bromleigh and moved on to a middle school. The home–school liaison teacher, a Punjabi and Urdu speaker, helps organise the group and facilitates conversation between mothers who speak Punjabi and the teachers of the deaf. She also raises white teachers' awareness of cultural differences and helps the session to run smoothly. Parents meet to learn BSL, to make communication between them and their children better and easier. They also take the opportunity to chat amongst each other. The Deaf Instructor teaches some sign language every week (vocabulary and phrases relevant to the children's current topic at school) and uses written English which will be translated for the parents into their home language. In effect many parents are learning two languages simultaneously.

The parents have been coming for a few years now and some have become proficient in BSL. Most still do not feel comfortable in the class-room, so the teachers take children's work into the parents' room. We are currently trying a variety of activities in which children and their parents can participate: for instance, when we had a topic on flowers children and parents produced collages showing flowers that grow in different seasons. We hope to encourage more parental involvement in the classroom as a means of supporting deaf children's development.

An acknowledgement of linguistic and cultural diversity

I mentioned earlier that the situation at Bromleigh School is linguisti-cally complex. BSL is made available to all children who need it to gain access to the curriculum. English is taught in spoken and written form as appropriate, because it is the language of mainstream education. It helps deaf children to communicate with hearing children and adults. Hearing children who have Punjabi as a home language have access to a bilingual

(Punjabi–English) support worker, but at the moment this provision does not extend to deaf children. Nor do we have any Deaf Instructors who are of Asian origin. The parents of one child asked if he could learn Pakistani Sign Language to gain insights into his own culture. So far, there has been no move by parents of deaf children in primary schools to have them taught Punjabi. The situation may change: we hope to employ additional bilingual (Punjabi–English) staff to work with the parents of deaf children, and also with the children themselves. This would enable us to include parents' and families' language and culture in Asian deaf children's education.

Equal Opportunities and the National Curriculum

Statemented pupils such as the eight deaf children at Bromleigh school can be exempted from the National Curriculum. But in Leeds there has been an attempt to adapt the National Curriculum rather than exempt children. *English For Ages 5 to 16* (the second 'Cox Report') mentions deaf children only once briefly in paragraph 12.14: deaf children '... might be allowed to use signing, or speech with signing support'. The report refers to deaf children's 'condition', implying a very clinical attitude. Clearly the National Curriculum presents difficult areas for deaf children, such as correct pronunciation for reading or the whole of Attainment Target 1 'Speaking and Listening'. How are these difficulties overcome?

The National Curriculum has been written for English children with English as their first spoken language. An exception is made for children in parts of Wales, who are not taught English formally until they are seven years old (after Key Stage 1 in the National Curriculum). Before that age the emphasis is on communicating in Welsh. For speakers of other languages, or for Welsh children living outside Wales, the National Curriculum gives no such assurances, nor does it for deaf children who use BSL as their first language.

Bilingual children who speak a language other than English at home may have the National Curriculum suspended for up to six months, on the understanding that after that time they will be able to compete on an equal level with their English speaking peers. During the SATs they are permitted to use their first language for subjects other than English, but they have no right to be taught these subjects in their first language and consequently their learning may be impeded[2]. They do not experience equal opportunities with monolingual English-speaking children.

In Leeds we have tried to promote full access to the National Curriculum to ensure equal opportunities for deaf children, but we have also argued that deaf children should be assessed in their first and naturally acquired language, BSL, where appropriate. A lot of work has gone into re-wording and breaking up into more detail the first English Attainment Target 'Speaking and Listening', the most problematical Attainment Target in the National Curriculum for deaf children. Deaf Instructors have collaborated in finding equivalent wordings for BSL, within a BSL attainment target. This has enabled them to assess a child's BSL skills. The reason for assessing deaf children's BSL is twofold: while they might 'underachieve' compared with their hearing peers in English, their equivalent BSL skills could prove to be age-equivalent. But also justification is given for delivering the National Curriculum in BSL and consequently giving deaf children equal access to teaching and assessment across the curriculum.

Teaching staff in the Hearing Impaired Service are currently working on another project to modify the modern languages curriculum to be used with deaf children. If the preferred first language of a deaf child is BSL, then English could be seen as that child's first modern foreign language. A lot more work needs to go into this project, but it appears to be a promising approach to ensure equal opportunities for deaf children, giving them 'entitlement' rather than 'exemption' from the National Curriculum.

Notes

1. To preserve anonymity I have used a pseudonym for the school I work in, as well as for any pupils mentioned.
2. Cummins (1984) reviews research on bilingual language learning and sets out the case for children learning initially through the language in which they are most proficient.

References

Cummins, J. (1984) *Bilingualism and Special Education: Issues in Assessment and Pedagogy*. Clevedon: Multilingual Matters.
Department of Education and Science/Welsh Office (DES/WO) (1989) *English for Ages 5 to 16*. London: HMSO (the second or final 'Cox Report').

Appendix: A Note on the Education of Deaf Children

This note has been compiled with help from Tony Booth from the School of Education at the Open University. For further information on British Sign Language, deaf culture, and the education of deaf children see the wide range of articles in Taylor & Bishop (1991) and its companion volume by Gregory & Hartley (1991).

The education of deaf children has been, and still is, a controversial issue in the UK. There are debates about whether deaf children should be taught alongside hearing children or in separate special schools, and also about what language should be used. Until recently oral approaches predominated: spoken English was used as the medium of education and the aim was to teach deaf children to communicate in spoken and written English. Those attending special schools learnt signing from each other outside the classroom. Sign language was frowned upon in education and its use was often formally prohibited.

Underlying oral approaches is the premise that deaf children need to communicate within a hearing community and that they should approximate to 'normal' (i.e. hearing) people as closely as possible. Such approaches tend to emphasise deafness as a disability or a communication deficiency. Oral approaches were also based on the belief that signing was a crude system that couldn't communicate complex ideas. It was only in the 1960s that British educators of the Deaf and academics acknowledged what Deaf people had long understood: that sign languages such as British Sign Language were full languages, on a par with spoken languages.[3]

Oral approaches were called into question partly because of the perceived educational failure of deaf children. Research carried out in the 1970s showed, for instance, that 50% of children with substantial hearing loss left school unable to read; deaf children who had been trained to lip read were no more proficient in this skill than hearing children who had not been specially trained; and the speech of many deaf children was difficult to understand (just under half the children attending schools for the deaf were very hard to understand or unintelligible (see Conrad (1979)). One response to such findings was to change oral approaches, which had been highly structured and formal, to make them conform more closely to 'natural' language acquisition. The new approach employed intensive exposure to spoken language and relied on improvements in hearing aid technology.

A more fundamental challenge to oralism came from the deaf community, whose members argued that oral approaches were discriminatory, denying deaf people the right to their own language and culture.

In the 1970s and 1980s sign systems began to be used in education to supplement English. At first, 'Signed English' was used — a sign system that translates English word order directly into sign. More recently bilingual approaches have been developed in which British Sign Language and English are introduced as separate languages. Bilingual approaches have been influenced by developments in bilingual education for children who speak languages other than English at home. They are premised on the belief that British Sign Language is similar to a hearing child's first language. While it is rarely chronologically a first language (unless a child has deaf parents) it is a language deaf children can learn easily and naturally (much as hearing children learn a spoken language). It is also a language in which deaf people can communicate without difficulty: they are not put at a disadvantage as they are with a spoken language. The belief, then, is that in school deaf children will learn more effectively through British Sign Language; British Sign Language will also provide access to English (as a second language); finally, and very importantly, British Sign Language provides access to the deaf community in Britain. Bilingual approaches acknowledge that deaf people are a cultural group and that Deaf culture is transmitted in part through the use of sign language.

References to Appendix

Conrad, R. (1979) *The Deaf School Child: Language and Cognitive Function.* London: Harper and Row.

Gregory, S. and Hartley, G. M. (1991) *Constructing Deafness.* London: Pinter Press, in association with The Open University.

Taylor, G. and Bishop, J. (1991) *Being Deaf: The Experience of Deafness.* London: Pinter Publishers, in association with The Open University.

4 Children Who Don't Stand Out

LYNDA YARD

There are four case studies in this chapter: case studies of well- behaved quiet children who, at first, seemed to melt into the background and were hard to get to know. Lynda Yard argues that children who don't stand out miss out on important aspects of education: it is hard to assess their needs and plan appropriate learning activities. The case studies show how careful observation helped their teachers get to know these children better, and also seemed to make the children themselves more confident.

The four children were all girls — a fact that may not seem surprising in the light of research that documents boys' dominance of classroom interaction. However, the relationship between unobtrusiveness and gender is not straightforward: Lynda argues that children are quiet or unobtrusive for different reasons, and their behaviour also varies in different contexts. The value of the chapter is that it encourages us to look beyond the more obvious social categories such as gender, 'race' and class, and towards issues that may be less easy to pigeon-hole, but that nevertheless affect children's experiences of education.

Introduction

'Sarah (Y4) had been in my class for a term and had not come to my particular notice for either behavioural or academic reasons. She was a quiet, well-behaved girl who seemingly came to school for one reason: to work. She did nothing to draw attention to herself either positively or negatively, maintained a fairly even standard of work and just merged into the background.' (Ann Read)

I'm sure this description will be familiar to other teachers. In any classroom there are the children who stand out (for several reasons) and who claim our time and attention. There are others, like Sarah, who seem to be getting on all right, give no cause for concern, and 'merge into the background'. James Pye (1988) called these 'invisible children'. He interviewed a number of young people after they had left school, and argues that those who had been 'invisible' had missed out on several aspects of schooling. Such children had not just been contentedly 'getting on with their work'. They had been resentful at being overlooked. They would have liked to participate more actively in classroom life, but lacked confidence. Some felt they had 'underachieved' in school — and, in fact, one or two whose performance had not been particularly noteworthy later developed the confidence to go on to higher education.

James Pye was interested in secondary schools, where it may seem easier for children not to be noticed simply because teachers see so many children during the week. But invisibility is also an issue in primary schools. Valerie Morgan and Seamus Dunn (1988) carried out observations in four nursery and infant classrooms. They found that all classes contained 'chameleons' who often passed unnoticed for considerable periods of time.

Invisibility became an issue recently for some primary teachers working in Croydon. A group of Croydon teachers involved in the National Oracy Project decided to make observations of the speaking and listening development of individual children over short periods of time, and write about these observations in case studies. Four of the teachers: Ann Coyle, Leonie Osborne, Brenda Pickles and Ann Read selected a child, like Sarah, who 'didn't stand out'. At the time I was a coordinator with the National Oracy Project, supporting the work of these and other teachers.

All four children were girls. This is in line with a great deal of research carried out in the classroom — for instance, Morgan & Dunn found that invisible pupils tended more often to be girls. However, I think it would be oversimplifying things to relate invisibility simply to gender. Children are likely to be quiet or unobtrusive for different reasons. The four teachers chose to study these children because they realised they knew very little about them. It was difficult to assess their knowledge and understanding through talk, and to plan appropriate learning activities. Would careful observation help teachers to know these children better and in so doing help them to have greater access to the curriculum? The National Curriculum requires children to make assessments of children's speaking and listening and, through their speaking and listening, of their conceptual development in other areas of the curriculum. Would this be possible in the case of children who didn't stand out?

The observations of the children were made during normal teaching time over a period of between two and four months, by the class teacher once or twice a week, less frequently by support teachers and occasionally by myself. Sometimes a tape recorder was used to record conversations and group discussions, but usually the teachers jotted down notes about the children's participation in selected activities.

Four Stories

Kate (Reception)

At the beginning of her observations Ann Coyle, Kate's teacher, wrote:

'Although Kate has progressed well academically in the two terms she has been with me, I felt there was a barrier between us and I had not really got to know her. She integrates with her peers alongside them rather than with them. There has been little verbal exchange or communication between Kate and her peers.'

Observations were made of Kate engaged in different classroom activities, working with and without an adult in small groups and with the whole class.

Extracts from Ann's notes show that Kate said little in class news time: 'When relating her news to the class she would only use one sentence and ... she was not very forthcoming'. She was similarly reticent in a group craft activity with the nursery nurse. Ann wondered if Kate was frightened of making a mistake or worried that she would fail to respond in a way that was acceptable to the teacher and her peers.

In two other activities, Kate was a more active participant. Ann's notes show that in the role play area: 'Kate participated, asked questions, initiated some of the play and was involved as much as the other children. She picked up a doll in the house and said "pretend this is my baby". She appeared happy, and was seen to be laughing and joking with the others'. In a discussion with the nursery nurse and Carol, her closest friend, Kate was again forthcoming. The picture story book *My Brother Sean* was shared and Kate began relating the story to her own experiences:

Kate: I used to go to this nursery — we all did, didn't we Carol?

N.N.:   Did you cry when you went to nursery?

Kate: No, because we had a really good slide and we played on it didn't we us three.

Ann felt Kate viewed this as a situation that was not threatening. Although questions were directed at Kate she was not under excessive pressure and the conversation flowed quite freely.

At a later point, during a group discussion with five other children and the teacher, something of a breakthrough occurred. At first, Kate said little, even when directly invited to comment. Then, the session ended and four of the children left the room. Ann also left briefly, and Kate and her friend Carol remained behind. The tape recorder, which had been recording the discussion, was still running. Ann's notes record what happened next:

'While I was away from the room Kate was completely relaxed and uninhibited. Kate and Carol were investigating the kitchen area. There were squeals of excitement when they thought they could hear me coming back. Kate quite openly told me they were looking in the kitchen and could see sugar. It was difficult to tell from the tape recording who initiated the investigation but Kate could be clearly heard to be excited.'

Ann felt that, up until this observation, Kate had shown little emotion — it was difficult to assess what she was feeling or thinking. Looking back on the period of study, Ann commented:

'Kate had been a passive and mainly quiet member of the class. She took a back seat and seemed happy for other children to take the lead. During the period of study Kate has released more of herself and a different Kate has emerged. ... The observations have helped me to build a clearer picture of her and her needs. ... I have learnt that groups need to be selected carefully to give children like Kate the opportunity to gain in confidence and I have come to the conclusion that there is a need for more spontaneous child-led talk and less teacher-directed questions and answers which Kate finds intimidating.'

Anita (Y2)

Anita's teacher, Leonie Osborne, was concerned that Anita didn't often talk voluntarily in small or large groups. She had to be asked direct questions, but seemed flustered and embarrassed by these and usually sat in silence. Even in a one-to-one situation with Leonie, Anita was reticent in expressing her ideas or points of view, and it was difficult to assess her understanding and knowledge through talk. Comments from other teachers showed that Anita's reticence had been noticed in Reception and Y1.

Leonie observed Anita in the playground and arriving at school, as well as in different classroom contexts. Leonie found that Anita played confidently with other children in the playground, taking care to involve a child on her own from another class.

On one occasion, in the classroom, Leonie gave Anita the task of explaining and playing a maths game on place value. Anita worked with several other children, one at a time. She was able to use mathematical language from a previous activity, and concentrated fully on the task. One child, who is not a good listener, began by saying:

Kate: I know what to do! (*Starting to deal the cards*).

Anita: It's a different game! You have to spread them out.

Anita was insistent that the other child follow the rules. She sometimes became frustrated but, on the whole, managed to remain patient and in control of the situation. Leonie found that, although she didn't say a great deal, Anita was successful in explaining the game and playing it with a variety of children, some of whom were not always cooperative. She also kept on task and was able to keep her partner's attention focused on the game.

Leonie tried out a role play activity with the whole class, based on a reading of the Pied Piper. The children, as townspeople of Hamelin, were voicing their concern about the rats at a council meeting. Anita was very quiet during this activity. Later, the children worked with a partner to draw and write down their ideas for a solution to the problem of the rats. Anita worked with a more dominant child, who did most of the writing and drawing. Leonie's notes show that Anita did contribute, however:

> [Anita] made sure that K drew the pictures but she herself gave directions as to what she should draw: 'Where are the rats going? I know, the rats are coming down the street ... Where are the ears? ... Only one ear?'

> When she felt K was taking too much time she said: 'Come on, I want to get this done'.

Leonie noticed that Anita's confidence as a speaker grew over the period of the study:

> 'She often came and told me things in the morning before school, sometimes about her family, sometimes about things she did with her friends. She was more relaxed in reading conferences and prepared to discuss what she had read ... She was also putting up her hand to answer questions in number activities with the whole class as we sat on the carpet together ...'

Leonie concluded:

> 'Anita was much more confident at expressing herself and more assertive than I had previously thought ... She was competent at giving instructions and in sharing ideas and making sure that work progressed without dominating others. Often she let others play a more active part whilst leading from behind ... There are several possible ways forward ... one is to build on her strengths in giving instructions and ask her to do this in larger groups extending the number of children she could work with.'

Lynn (Y4)

Lynn attended a school for pupils with moderate learning difficulties. Her teacher, Brenda Pickles, wanted to establish her level of spoken English in a number of different contexts. She observed Lynn in the playground; chatting with other children about their work; taping her news (with Brenda); and working in a group of four and with the whole class.

Brenda found that Lynn contributed little in certain contexts. For instance, her taped news was very brief and she didn't share anything personal or that really mattered in class news time (news of a new baby was communicated quietly to Brenda *after* news time). Brenda decided to ask the children to discuss their news in groups without the teacher, and told the children to help each other by asking questions. In this context Lynn was much more forthcoming, asking questions to draw out other children:

M: Yeah, I went on those twice with my sister and my dad won me a couple of things on the guns and that.

Lynn: And what was that then?

J: What did your sister do?

M: She just went on a couple of rides and he won me a couple of things on the guns and that. My dad.

Lynn: So what was that he won on the gun?

M: He won me a couple of things. I won a coconut on the coconut shy.

Lynn: What else?

In another context, when using Multi-link to make shapes, Lynn worked well with others in her group and was able to settle minor disputes:

J: I'm going to join lots together.

M: We all do it together.

J: Well, I'm going to do it this way.

M: That's not right.

Lynn: We should work together but it's OK if she doesn't. Let's do the bottom first.

Brenda commented on the observations:

'I do not know if she has developed or if I was not giving her the chance to show her full potential until I let them do their news in groups ... I will now organise the class so that children are given the opportunity to show their potential and skills to the full.'

Sarah (Y4)

Ann Read, Sarah's teacher, wrote at the beginning of her observations:

'Sarah never spoke out in class or contributed to our discussion. She answered questions which were directed at her, usually correctly, and only spoke to me about her work. As the academic year was progressing I felt that I was beginning to know many of the other children in the class. The majority would chat to me socially at the beginning of the day or when I was in the playground but Sarah didn't and I therefore felt I wasn't learning about her ... I wanted to see why she was a reluctant talker and how to overcome this.'

As with the other children observations of Sarah were made by the teacher, support teacher and occasionally by myself in a range of contexts.

Sarah clearly understood the work she was doing, but seemed to lack confidence and to follow the lead of other children. One one occasion, Ann watched Sarah as she worked with her friend Ruth on a maths activity, trying to decide how many different nets there were for a cube:

'Sarah ... let Ruth lead her through the activity. There was little verbal exchange. Sarah recorded her work, looking frequently to Ruth's piece of paper. (Would more talk have been promoted if they had been asked to record together on one piece of paper?) When I asked them what they'd discovered, Ruth said: 'We've found ten different ways'. Sarah however had been looking intently at her paper and said: 'But some of them are the same but only the other way round'. This was an important observation and very relevant to the activity. Sarah understood the nature of the task and it was interesting that although she knew she was drawing the same net from a different angle and not a different net at all, she made no reference to this during the activity to her partner, nor did it have any bearing on her method of recording.'

On another occasion, Sarah confidently explained to me the work she was about to begin on map coordinates, then moved to another table and sat next to Ruth. I noted with some surprise that Sarah proceeded to listen while Ruth explained what they were to do and wrote only what Ruth suggested. Clearly, Sarah knew what to do before she sat down — so why had she felt the need to adopt her familiar role of being 'led' through a task? Ann speculated that it would be easier for Sarah to continue in her accustomed role than to change — she was doing what was expected of her.

At a later point in the study, Ann observed Sarah taking part in an art activity with a small group of children, including Ruth. Ann was also taking part in the activity:

'We looked at an impressionist painting by the artist Claude Monet: we discussed how the artist had used 'light' and 'colour' in his picture to create an effect. Although the tape was running it did not seem to inhibit the children at all. They spoke naturally and clearly, picked up on ideas and suggestions offered by their peers. I took part in the discussion and painted alongside them when we came to the practical part of the activity.'

'Initially Sarah listened while other children commented on the painting, then she joined in the discussion with no prompting from anyone. This was the first time she had ever done this, in my presence anyway. The discussion continued with all of us contributing equally. All ideas were considered, no-one's suggestions were ridiculed and everyone seemed at ease:

Daren: He hasn't painted anything on the face.

Teacher: Why do you think that is?

Sarah: There isn't any detail.

Paul: He's used lots of colour for the flowers.

Sarah: They're just lines of colour.

Teacher: Do they make you think of flowers?

All: Yes.

Sarah: I think it's a windy day because her scarf is blowing out.

Daren: And it's raining because she's holding an umbrella.'

Later still, while carrying out a traffic survey outside school, Sarah seemed more confident and relaxed, and laughed and joked with other children. Ann commented that, given the right opportunities, Sarah would be able to participate more actively. Furthermore, she seemed to be developing greater confidence:

'Over the period of study, Sarah was showing signs of changing from a shy, introverted girl, to one who laughs and jokes. She is beginning to talk to me more, both on and off task and in a talk-related activity she is beginning to relax, look comfortable and contribute.'

Conclusions

These are four individual stories, and it would be unwise to generalise too much from them. However there are one or two common threads that seem to run through each account.

All four girls were seen, at the beginning of the period of study, to be children who communicated rarely with the teacher or with their peers. All four were law-abiding children, anxious to follow the rules of the classroom and anxious not to make mistakes in their work. All grew in confidence during the period of study and were seen to talk more with their peers and with their teachers. What happened?

First, each teacher began to recognise situations which were particularly difficult for these children: whole-class newstime, group and one-to-one activities with the teacher in which tasks were specific and teacher-led, and whole-class role play with the teacher.

At the same time, each teacher began to recognise and give increased time and opportunity for situations in which these children *did* find it possible to communicate. These are worth noting as it is possible that a greater emphasis on similar situations would benefit other children who 'don't stand out'.

Situations in which children communicated confidently included role play areas without the teacher and situations outside the classroom (Kate and her friend in the kitchen and Anita doing a traffic survey). In the classroom, situations in which the children communicated confidently included speaking to the teacher or another adult when in the position of *expert* (Sarah explained her work on Maths coordinates to me, an outsider; Kate told the nursery nurse about her nursery school experiences). In a group with the teacher Sarah spoke confidently in a situation in which there was no one right answer and where all contributions, including those of the teacher, were equally valid (the discussion of the Monet painting).

It may be of particular interest to note two instances of ways in which teachers built on the law-abiding, rule-following features of these children. Brenda gave Lynn's group clear instructions that they were to ask each other questions in their group news-telling. Given this framework Lynn evidenced skills of encouraging and even goading other children to speak. Leonie taught Anita a mathematical game and then asked her to teach it to several groups of children. She did so confidently and competently allowing for no deviations from the rules of the game.

Children like Kate, Anita, Lynn and Sarah are difficult to observe. Pye noted the secondary teachers he interviewed admitted that they responded more readily to children who made contact with them; in any interaction it is easier to respond to people who make eye contact, who smile back.

Children who 'don't stand out' are perhaps striving so intently to follow the rules of the classroom that they are unable to respond to those who are perceived as makers of the rules. All four children were observed communicating confidently away from the classroom and in the classroom when the rules were clearly understood: taking part in group discussions when children had been told to ask each other questions; in group discussions where it was clear there was no one right answer; talking to another adult about an area in which the child was the expert.

The four teachers in this article persevered and made determined efforts to know their invisible children. They noticed and began to plan for situations in which the children found it less threatening to make contact with others and, in two instances, built positively on the law-abiding features of the children. Four happier, more confident children emerged, children who became increasingly easier to observe as they began to talk more readily in formal and informal situations. These children will now have full access to the National Curriculum as teachers will be able to assess their understanding and knowledge through talk.

Acknowledgements

Thanks are due to the following Croydon teachers: Ann Coyle (Good Shepherd R.C. Primary), Leonie Osborne (Asburton Infant), Brenda Pickles (St. Nicholas) and Ann Read (Elmwood Junior).

References

Morgan, V. and Dunn, S. (1988) Chameleons in the classroom: Visible and invisible children in nursery and infant classrooms. *Educational Review* 40 (1), 3–12.
Pye, J. (1988) *Invisible Children*. Oxford: Oxford University Press.

5 Working with Traveller Children

This chapter consists of a number of contributions from different people — two workers with Traveller families, a Traveller child and two adult Travellers writing about their experiences with schools.

Travellers are a minority group who regularly suffer not just from stereotyping and isolated prejudice but from institutionalised racism. The position of their children in school can be very fraught. In his contribution Brian Foster points out that Travellers are by no means an homogeneous group; he offers background information to help understand some of the Traveller families who may join a school community.

Andrew Pritchard is an advisory teacher for Traveller education. His contribution is a positive, practical and optimistic account of a project designed to defuse an unpleasant situation which had resulted when some Traveller children joined an Ealing school.

We also have the personal voices of three Travellers. Siobhan was interviewed a year or so ago when she was still in primary school by Liz Laing, a teacher working with London Travellers. The other pieces come from a book which Liz Laing has compiled, working with Traveller women. Bridget Gaffey, now in her twenties, describes her primary school experience in Ireland about 15 years ago and Kathleen Joyce tells how Traveller children were excluded from a school Christmas party. These stories make apparent the importance of a proper school policy about welcoming Travellers and recognising their special circumstances. They alert us to the possibility that Travellers — both children and parents — may have had damaging experiences in the past which need to be understood and counteracted.

Equal Opportunities for Traveller Children

BRIAN FOSTER

Introduction

Travellers represent a small minority within the community and within our schools. But the issues raised when Traveller children go into school are neither minor, nor of relevance only to the minority. They test out the response of the education system at every level in equal opportunities, with respect to access, curriculum, anti-racism and home–school liaison. If a school is sufficiently flexible to respond constructively to the educational needs of Travellers, then it is likely to be doing a good job with most of its other pupils too.

Culture and change

Travellers in Britain are not an homogeneous group. There are Romanies who belong to a racial group who originated in Northern India and have migrated through Asia and Europe over a period of 1000 years; they arrived in Britain in the 16th century since when their migration has continued to the United States, South America and Australia. There are also Travellers who come from indigenous communities such as Irish and Scottish Tinkers, which have an equally long nomadic tradition and a wide range of migration. In addition to these traditional nomadic communities there are also economic and occupational Travellers, such as circus and fairground workers, and groups broadly described as new Travellers, who have become nomadic to develop alternative lifestyles and/or because of pressures such as unemployment and homelessness. The focus of this chapter is on the traditional Traveller communities but it should be understood that there is an equally strong case to be made for the recognition of the way of life and culture of other Travellers.

The history, traditions and experiences of each Traveller family will shape their beliefs and values, and generalisations can be dangerous. But there do seem to be four priorities which characterise the difference between Travellers and the settled population, specifically the maintenance of extended family networks and community contacts, a positive attitude to mobility, a tradition of self-education and the perpetuation of a shared language. Teachers might bear these in mind at the early stages of a developing relationship with Traveller children in school.

Traveller camps are not random groups of individual families in individual trailers; each camp will have one or more extended family groups and, if space allows, the trailers will be arranged to enclose an identifiable area of land. In practical terms children grow up in a large, close-knit community, surrounded by grandparents, aunts, uncles, cousins and siblings. This community offers care, support and education, and can help share and dissipate the tensions which prejudice and hostility can generate.

Although different extended family groups may compete for work and places on sites, Travellers also share an overarching sense of community as a system of support and sharing, and a mechanism for bestowing approval and status. The landmarks of family life, christenings, weddings, funerals etc. are also communal events, through which respect is shown and identity reinforced. Information is exchanged, alliances established, matches made, which in turn contribute to the perpetuation of the community and the culture. Horse fairs and races, such as Appleby, Epsom, Ballinasloe and Puck, are communal meeting points, whose social value is at least as significant as their stated purpose.

Mobility is no longer an economic necessity for most families, but nomadism is positively valued. Travellers from houses or official sites often travel out in trailers to the horse fairs or the hopfields as a summer vacation. For Traveller children security and stability are represented not by a locality, land or property, but by family and community, which are always with them.

Traditionally Travellers have passed on their own specialised skills to their children, usually informally as they go about their everyday business. Few Travellers regard formal education as a threat to their culture. Educated Travellers are well respected within the community and there is ample historical evidence to show that they have sought education for their children wherever this was practicable. However, the lack of formal education is not looked down on, since Travellers recognise not only that there are many reasons beyond an individual's control why they might have been denied access and opportunity, but also that survival and economic skills are not necessarily dependant on it. Formal schooling is only part of Traveller children's wider education.

Both Romany and Celtic Travellers have their own languages, though for most families in Britain they do not constitute a mother tongue; both parents and children have a full command of English while their knowledge and use of their own language may be quite superficial. Politicised Irish Travellers are keen that their language should not be lost and are considering teaching it to their children as a second language. They see the suppression of their language as part of a wider oppression and its reclamation as an important assertion of cultural identity. Romanes is the mother tongue of many European Rom, and their children grow up functionally bilingual with the language of the country they live in. Very few English

Romanies can speak the language as well as their European counterparts, but their continued awareness of the language contributes to the group's sense of identity.

Foundations of equal opportunities

Educational opportunity for Travellers cannot be separated from other basic human rights, particularly the right to stay in one place. Less than half the Travellers in England and Wales have places on official sites. A substantial, but unknown, proportion of Travellers are in housing on either a permanent or temporary basis. The rest live on unauthorised camps and suffer considerable instability and insecurity. Usually the process of eviction begins as soon as they move onto a piece of land and they may have to move on almost immediately. Compulsory movement under these circumstances has nothing to do with nomadism. Eviction serves only to disrupt the families' lives and causes alienation and depression. Unauthorised camps are often dangerous and unsuitable, usually without basic facilities such as water, sanitation and refuse collection. They can be quite large, since the families have no real choice about where they stop and no right to prevent other equally desperate families from pulling on beside them. Families camping in small groups are vulnerable to attack by racists, but large camps tend to be more disorganised and threatening to the settled community, which in turn generates pressures for early eviction. The frequency of eviction disrupts all aspects of Travellers' lives.

In educational terms this insecure life means substantial numbers of school places are needed on a short term basis, demands which cannot always be met. Adults and children face problems in gaining access to a whole range of health and welfare provision. The stress and disruption associated with frequent evictions cause economic and social hardship, which can affect the child's capacity to benefit from schooling. One group of families with whom we work has had to move 14 times in 18 months; although they have never moved beyond a five mile radius, they have spent time in five different London boroughs. On a few occasions their children have been able to go into school but normally it has been for short periods and unsurprisingly their educational progress has been limited. Children with special needs have not been fully assessed. Among these families are literate parents seeing their children growing up unable to read.

During the 1980s enlightened councils began to question policies designed to keep Traveller families on the move. They recognised that, all too often, they would go through the expensive and unpleasant process of eviction only to push the families onto another piece of council-owned land. It was a time when anti-racism and women's issues were high on the

Aa Astral

I could tell you how I know.

It has four windows.
It has chrome jacks.
It is very long.

It is a nice trailer

One day
I was walking down the country.
I saw an Astral trailer.

1

2

Kk kettle

We put it on our stove
and it boils away.

We have a kettle
and we have a trailer.

We have a stove
in our trailer
and we have

a big black kettle

7

8

Some examples from *Alphabet Stories*, produced by Teachers for Travellers, London

political agenda, and Travellers, teachers, health workers and other professionals began to make the case for non-harassment policies, whereby families would not be moved unnecessarily and problems could be resolved by dialogue rather than tow-trucks. The political pendulum has swung several times since then and the remaining non-harassment policies have a precarious existence.

The benefits of non-harassment policies for education are clear; where Travellers have more stability, they have far better opportunities for education. In Southwark, for example, increasing numbers of Traveller children from tolerated camps are getting places in nursery schools, with benefits for their primary schooling. Greater stability and positive primary experience contributes to successful transfer to secondary schools. A Traveller women's writing group has also formed and the women involved have taken part in INSET for teachers and inspectors, which all contributes to mutual understanding.

The Blair Peach Middle School 'Moving Along' Project: Autumn 1991

ANDREW PRITCHARD

Blair Peach Middle School is situated in the Southall area of the west London borough of Ealing. Southall has a large population of families of Asian origin and Ealing Council uses the district to temporarily house Traveller families who have found themselves, for one reason or another, in need of accommodation, often because of the insufficient provision for caravan dwellers in West London. Most of the families are committed to a travelling lifestyle and do not remain in settled, housed accommodation for long. The children of two of these Traveller families attend Blair Peach Middle School. Despite a sympathetic approach, and many efforts to integrate the children, the staff found themselves unused to the culture and mores of travelling society and sought support from the recently-established, but under-funded, Ealing Travellers' Education Service.

I am the only teacher employed as full-time support for Travellers in the borough of Ealing: I work 0.5 in one First and Middle school which serves the official caravan site and has 36 Traveller children on roll, and 0.5 as peripatetic support for all phases of education across the borough. To date, I have identified 121 Traveller children attending Ealing schools.

At the request of the Head of Blair Peach, I visit the school whenever time allows. I made contact with the three middle school Traveller children she had on roll in the Autumn of 1991 — all from one family I had previously worked with when they had been trailer-based on the official caravan site. I suggested that the Head also admit the children from another recently-housed Traveller family needing help in finding a school. We thought that it would help if the Traveller children were less isolated. However, the situation deteriorated to such an extent that one of the Traveller boys, reflecting local tensions, found himself in continual and direct conflict with the school and was regarded as a disruptive element in an otherwise harmonious and well-administered school. The Head and I decided that a long-term strategy was necessary. In the short-term, we reluctantly agreed to exclude one of the Traveller boys to prevent the situation deteriorating beyond rescue point.

Blair Peach Middle is an open-plan school where the children are used to working in a variety of different groupings; the Head and I decided that we would create a group of mixed gender, age and ability, including the four remaining Traveller children. We also included those children who had been involved in the 'trouble' previously. The other children represented the age/gender/ethnic mix of the children attending the school. There were twelve children in the group and we planned, initially, a series of six two-hour, weekly, sessions. We were given the design and technology area to work in. Our undeclared aims were to promote discussion about differing lifestyles, to encourage the ability to work collaboratively, to increase literacy levels, and to incorporate the Traveller culture into the ethos of the school.

I was surprised at the willingness with which the children launched themselves into the project — as if they had been expecting 'something to happen' as a result of the succession of 'unusual' occurrences since the Traveller children had been attending.

I introduced myself as a teacher who visited various schools to work with groups of children on negotiated areas of study, using at times potentially hazardous equipment. The children were suitably impressed by the obvious danger when I activated a small electric jig-saw I had brought with me. I was anxious not to give the impression that the children were 'in trouble', or 'not to be trusted' — hence the introduction of equipment requiring a degree of maturity and skill to operate safely and successfully. The potential danger of the jig-saw allowed me to talk about the need for care and consideration to ensure personal and general safety and well-being.

I steered the discussion towards more general considerations of the needs of others, asking the children to think about the differences that existed between us. We had a long list. I encouraged the children, particularly the Travellers (whom I knew from previous visits to the school), to talk about as many differing lifestyles as they could think of — finally focusing on the nomadic choice. The group agreed to use this as a starting point for our work together — and named the project 'Moving Along'.

Because of the recent difficulties in co-existence, in the initial session I asked the children to work individually on deciding what they would pack into a personal suitcase for an extended journey. After they had made their individual choices and recorded things which involved some complicated and unexpected perspective drawing, the children agreed on what they would collectively need and packed a 'group' suitcase. This was their first collaborative activity.

Subsequent sessions extended the theme. Using electric tools, building kits, batteries, motors and an assortment of materials such as polystyrene, cardboard and glue the children produced increasingly complex working models of vehicles — and contents — that they deemed essential as they 'Moved Along'. There were not enough tools and equipment for everyone to use simultaneously, so I introduced smaller groups to ensure fairness. This gave me the opportunity to break up the 'natural' cliques and to spread the Traveller children throughout the groups.

With the opportunity to display their knowledge of engines, gear systems and the like, the Traveller children's status rose noticeably — contradicting many previously held stereotypes. It was a testimony to the good sense of children that in this supportive environment completing a task in the best possible way became paramount.

Discussion work was an important part of every session — although sometimes children were reluctant to talk about feelings and emotions. Also, the bilingual children needed an input of specific vocabulary to explain their emotions in English. But there was enormous ingenuity when the children were asked to communicate without actually talking. This activity arose from acting out arriving in a new and foreign place and communicating immediate needs to people who did not share any languages the children could collectively call on. Faced with this dilemma one boy disappeared from the room and returned five minutes later with a tray of sand from the Nursery and drew rapid representations of his requirements with his forefinger!

As the children shared more positive experiences, their confidence in each other grew and they ventured more 'real' information about themselves. Some of the Asian children described experiences and feelings of being 'strangers in a strange land'. It was a turning point in the direction of the group when the Traveller children, reluctantly at first, admitted to identifying with the feelings described by their Asian peers.

At the time of writing, the project is still being developed. I have been struck throughout by the apparent natural willingness of the children to accept, tolerate, and understand. I intend to introduce the notion that the true origins of the Traveller culture are to be found in Asia, further challenging some of the children's prejudices. A Traveller mother, newly arrived in the area from Ireland, on seeing a large, public Asian wedding declared that were it not for the preponderance of saris and other ethnic dress she could have believed herself back home at a Traveller celebration!

10 trailers on a ground

From *Alphabet Stories*, produced by Teachers for Travellers, London

One of the girls in the group undertook — using one of the school's BBC computers — to produce a written record of every session. I have produced- learning materials incorporating some of these ideas which, along with other resources, are available from the Ealing Traveller Education Project. (see 'Resources' section).

Siobhan: Starting School (transcribed from a conversation with Liz Laing)

Well — my first day at school — all my class had a PE lesson and I had no shorts or top and I couldn't do it and I felt all left out and alone. When I first came to this school this girl was very kind enough to show me around and show me how the pips work and where the library is and the toilets and everywhere like that and — um when its dinner-time you have to line up for a good ten minutes and I felt very funny lining up for the first time.

... Well, people starts calling me gypsy and telling me I don't know how to wash myself and I says to them, 'can you wash yourself?' — they says 'yeah' — well I says, 'you're all right then aren't you and — um — you'd better go home and get a bath for yourself 'cos you needs it 'cos you're very dirty'. They says to me, 'well at least we live in a house anyhow'. Yeah and I says, 'at least I live in a trailer and I'm proud of that as well'. I says, 'there's nothing to be ashamed of that' I said — 'I'm proud of that' I said, 'reared and born in a trailer' I said, 'and I'm proud of it'. And then me and this girl was arguing over — she was calling me names, and I missed school one day and when I came back I was hearing it all round that this girl said that I punched her, that I gave her a box into the mouth, but I never touched her and she nearly got me in trouble as well with the teachers, but she didn't. ... Sometimes we gets towed off, off the camps for no reason, we keeps it clean, does everything we can like to keep it clean, and the council and the police just comes down for no reason and just tells us to get off there, 'we don't want you' that's what they say to you sometime and the people always complain and we does nothing to them. They just puts you off for nothing.

... The teachers are very nice here, now Mrs Jackson, she's a very nice teacher right, she helps you with your work actually but I thinks that if I don't get it right she might give out to me, but I tries, you know, really tries to get it right and sometimes I really do get it right, but if I don't get it right she don't even mind, she just helps me with it, along the way, and she's always interested.

Bridget Gaffey: School Experiences in Dundalk in the Late 1970s

I went to school in Dundalk. When all the girls were learning Maths and English, Irish and History I was given a colouring book to go to the back of the class while all the other girls of the settled community did the work. They never tried to teach me any of the things I would have loved to have done, like play music and PE. I have never done anything like that. My reading and writing were picked up, not in schools, but off a nun. I used to go for two hours every morning. Myself and one more boy were all she was teaching because we were getting taught confirmation. That's where I learned what I know. I really would love to have stayed on at school but I left school at twelve years of age so I missed out on a lot of learning. I am now married and have two children and I am very happy with life, thank God, but I still feel I would love to have learned more about science, photography, history, medicine and cookery. I would love to be able to understand a lot. Now I feel it's too late to learn and pass exams.

I left school at twelve because we were moving about a lot. And I must have been at about ten schools since I started at about the age of five.

Kathleen Joyce: Christmas Time in a Primary School in Buckinghamshire 1986

There were six small Travelling children going to the primary school. They were going to their school for about six months before Christmas. They came home one day and told me that they had to bring some stuff for the Christmas party. So all the mums gave the children some crisps, drinks and fruit for the party. We didn't find out till they came home that they had the settled children in one room and the Traveller children in another room. I think that was a terrible thing to happen to our children and the children themselves were very disappointed that there were only six of them in that party.

Acknowledgement

We are grateful to Liz Laing for allowing us to draw on her work.

Resources

(1) The following are all available from Traveller Education Team, c/o Ilderton School, Varcoe Road, London SE16 3LA, Telephone 071 237 1174:

The following children's books written by Denis Longmore: *Robot Goes to School, Travellers from the Stars, I Could Have Been...*, and *Mary and Kizzy*.

Laing, L. (ed.) (1992) *Moving Stories: Traveller Women Write*. Inner London Traveller Education Team in association with Southwark Council.

(2) Other resources including material which can be used with children:

Cannon, J. (1989) *Travellers: An Introduction*. London: Interchange Books.

Department of Education (1985) *Education of Travellers' Children*. London: HMSO.

Hatfield Polytechnic (1992) *The Education of Gypsy and Traveller Children: Action-research and Co-ordination*. The Publications Office, Library and Media Services Department, Hatfield Polytechnic, College Lane, Hatfield AL10 9AD.

Gmelch, S. (1986) *Nan: The Life of an Irish Travelling Woman*. London: Souvenir Press (Reprinted 1987 by Pan, London).

Hunter, M. (1985) *I'll Go My Own Way (A Contemporary Novel for Young Adults)*. London: Hamish Hamilton.

Kenrick, D. and Bakewell, S. (1990) *On the Verge: The Gypsies of England*. London: Runnymede Trust.

Moving Home: A Primary School Topic. Peterborough Centre for Multicultural Education, 165a Cromwell Road, Peterborough PE1 2EL.

Moving On. Photopack available from Minority Rights Group, 379 Brixton Road, London SW9 7DE.

Reiss, C. (1975) *The Education of Traveller Children*. London: MacMillan.

(3) The West Midlands Education Service for Travelling Children, Broad Lanes, Bilston, West Midlands WV14 0SB (Telephone: Bilston 353925) has pioneered much work with Travelling children in the UK and is always willing to give assistance.

(4) A directory of contacts in South East Region Traveller Education can be obtained from H. Gladbaum, Teachers' Centre, Harrow, Tudor Road, Wealdstone, Middlesex (price £2).

(5) For further information about resources he uses in work with Traveller children, Andrew Pritchard can be contacted at Travellers' Education, Resources and Inset Centre, John Perryn School, Acton, London W3 7PD, Tel: 081 743 5648, and Ealing Professional Centre, Westlea Road, Hanwell, London W7, Tel: 081 840 4050, ext 32.

6 Looking Back: Teenage Girls' Recollections

Memories of their primary school experiences are still vivid for the five girls who contributed to this chapter. Many of their recollections are very positive, but as teenagers they are beginning to make connections between the personal and the political, and each writes in a different way about issues of gender, race and power. They discuss trying to fit in at school, coping with racism, and challenging the power of boys. Sofia has experienced being both bully and victim, and Sheli writes about feeling alone, and unsupported. Each girl found some ways of asserting her own power, and her own personal identity, but there is a strong sense that they would have liked more help from teachers, and from the school, in relation to dealing with sexist, racist and bullying behaviour. They wanted more support in becoming aware of their own, and of other children's cultural identities.

Sofia Choudhary (16)

Now, at the age of sixteen, I look back on my primary school years and realise that I had a whale of a time. This was because I was one of the more popular, well-liked children at school. I used to really look forward to getting to school for yet another fun packed day. I was familiar with the local area because both my infants and nursery schools were situated close by. This made me feel completely at home within these surroundings. My school was very mixed — there were a lot of cultures in it, there were

65

black, white and Asian children, amongst others. But having lots of cultures in a school doesn't necessarily mean that you learn to appreciate these cultures, as I now realise.

There are ways in which I feel my school could have been improved, as I now feel that there were areas of injustice and unfairness. For instance, in assemblies we used to sing songs and recite the Lord's Prayer, this was unfair as it meant we were only being taught the Christian religion. If the time was used constructively we could have learnt about all the cultures and religions, hence making the school more of an understanding community.

Please don't mistake what I'm saying and think that the school was completely 'anti-culture' because we did have 'special' assemblies, where we learnt about celebrations such as Eid and Hannukah. The only problem was that these assemblies were too infrequent. They needed to occur more often in order to make the school a more integrated unit. In order to develop our knowledge to the fullest, we need to learn about other cultures and appreciate other peoples' ways of lives, besides our own.

Because of the lack of support shown in school to bring out other cultures, I found myself trying to be very 'English' at school, even though I am Asian. I never used to wear Shalwar Kameez to school and I had a short bobbed haircut. I remember girls in my class saying 'Sofia, you're not like the other Asian girls, you're "different"'. By 'different' they meant I wasn't what was at the time a typical stereotyped Asian girl. That is, someone who is quiet and timid, too embarrassed to say or do anything. I wanted to tell them that all Asian girls weren't like that but I never did, I was just glad that they liked me and I was happy enough to settle for that. Okay, so maybe the Asian girls in my class *were* timid and quiet and perhaps I was different because I played football and always had something to say for myself but I think that these other girls would have opened up more if only they had been taught that it's alright to belong to a different culture. It would have been very interesting to learn about other peoples' cultures. After all, a bit of variation never did anyone any harm.

During most of the four years I spent in primary school, I belonged to what I thought at the time was a really 'cool' gang, which used to make other peoples' lives a misery. Yep — in other words, we were bullies. Our gang, which was called The Pink Panthers consisted of nine girls: a black girl, who was the leader; two white girls, three mixed race girls and three Asian girls. The gang leader was a girl called Lorna and everyone was terrified of her and hated her. I don't know why we were so scared of her; she wasn't bigger than any of us or stronger. As Lorna was nice to us, we used to help her make everyone else's life a misery. After all, it is said that

'If you can't beat them, join them'. So that's exactly what we did because it was easier than standing up for ourselves.

I still, to this day cannot understand why she had such an overwhelming control over us and she also managed to wrap all the boys around her little finger. I'm surprised that Lorna had so much confidence because people who have something wrong with their physical appearance usually lack confidence and Lorna had severe eczema, which scarred and dried up her skin. She also had very little hair, but nobody took the mickey out of her, and she was as confident as one could possibly want to be.

Yet there was a boy called David in our class who looked different because he was rather overweight and he was constantly picked on. He also had a weak bladder and stumbled when he spoke — that gave us an excuse to say spiteful things to him. We used to push him around and say horrible things like he's a baby because he wets his bed and we used to imitate the way he spoke. I can't remember the teachers ever telling us off for being horrible to him. Maybe that was because we never actually used to hit him or bully him enough to make him cry — but surely the teachers were aware that something was going on? We should have been made to realise how malicious and spiteful we were. I feel really ashamed of myself now. That boy David must've dreaded coming to school everyday and *nobody* should be scared to come to school.

I feel that the reason why the Pink Panthers were bullies was that we were victims of a bully ourselves — and that bully was Lorna. If a teacher had asked us why we bully people I think that we would have said 'It's Lorna, Miss. If she doesn't like somebody then we don't because we're scared of her'.

The time for me to stop bullying others came when I, myself, was a victim of my gang. Finally I had a taste of my own medicine. For some reason I broke up with Lorna and that meant that most of the class didn't like me either. I remember feeling lonely and restless, because there was no-one to play with or talk to. My so-called friends didn't actually physically bully me — there was only the occasional nudge with the elbow when they walked past. The punishment they gave me, which I think in some ways was worse, was sending me to Coventry. Everybody ignored me and it was horrid. I think that I may have preferred it if they actually said things to my face so that I could stand up for myself but they never did, they only made spiteful remarks and conversations about me that were within earshot.

Sarah Davis (15)

Being in an all girls school for the past five years, I haven't experienced any of the frustration I felt in my primary school when boys and girls were treated differently. Everything seemed to be ruled by stereotypes. For instance, at break-times the playground would be taken over by the boys for their games of football, leaving the girls with the remaining spaces around the painted boundaries of the football pitch. We girls would be annoyed at this arrangement but most of us would shy away from confronting the boys so we would put up with it.

I think at the time we accepted it, not only because it happened with the three other year groups in the school, but because football was seen as a man's game and therefore it was logical that they would want to play it — even if it meant them taking over the playground. These beliefs were only reinforced when a football club was started for the boys and the girls were given a netball club.

It didn't occur to us to complain to the teachers because we were sure that if they had felt we were being treated unfairly, they would have intervened and it wasn't until I got to my senior school that I realised that if you want something to be noticed, you have to point it out yourself, or it will be ignored.

Nicola Darvill (15)

At primary school I was in a class of twenty five, thirteen of whom were boys. I was able to mix with both boys and girls and the class was like one happy family. We all accepted that some could pick up new skills quicker than others and there was no ill feeling toward any member of the class because of his or her capability.

That was until Chris arrived. Chris came into our class in the third year of junior school. As we had been together for three years already, Chris was instantly an outsider. He made no attempt to get to know any of the girls in the class and it was soon discovered that he had a very chauvinistic attitude.

Chris was given tests and papers to determine his level of work. (Each subject was graded using colour codes. In maths we worked from SMP cards which were coded into six different coloured boxes which we worked from over the four years at junior school. Each colour was for different abilities.) At that time I would have been put in the category of 'top student'. I was on the hardest box and I found learning very easy. However this caused no problems and there was no resentment from any other child.

It was soon discovered that Chris was a very intelligent boy. He was put to work on the same books and boxes as I was and I had hoped that this would mean a friendship between us. I was soon shown that this meant nothing of the sort. Chris' chauvinistic attitude came shining through.

He began to make remarks about 'Girls not belonging at the top of the class' and how '... a women's place was in the home not at school'. I think he meant a lot of what he said even though it was put into a sarcastic tone. At first his comments were taken with a pinch of salt and his spiteful phrases were not so effective. It was then that Chris changed his tactics.

Chris was a dominating person. He was very much a 'leader' and liked to be in charge of people. His new amusement was to work on destroying my self esteem and at the same time boost his confidence. Chris' new strategy was to get all of the boys on his side. He used his power to rally the boys in our class, and made his comments a game. It was now seen as fun to pick on me and to be chauvinistic. He made everything a competition between us. For every piece of work set it was the same routine: either to finish first or to achieve the best marks. It was OK and I could handle it. But when he added the comments and the constant competing, the pressure all became too much.

It was non-stop torment. The new angle was that as a girl I wasn't able to compete ... and now Chris had the boys involved as well. He was the leader and he had power. The girls, being loyal, stood by me and although no words or fights took place there began a silent feud. The atmosphere changed from being warm and friendly to cold spitefulness. Where I felt uncomfortable Chris thrived on it. Eventually the weak side of me gave in and I allowed Chris to overtake me on all school work.

I felt trapped. I had now dug myself deep into Chris' little hole as the girls in the class began to resent me for letting them down. My work suffered and my grades dropped. By now I had such a low picture of myself that I believed maybe this was where I deserved to be, where I belonged. Just as Chris had told me.

But I sat down and thought about what I had done by admitting defeat and giving in to Chris. He was now an idol for the boys to copy and follow, he had succeeded in both splitting up our happy class, and most importantly, he had made my work suffer. By giving in to his bullying I had proved to the boys that I was weak, just as girls should be. It was the stubbornness and the fighting side of my nature that won me over this time. I realised I wasn't prepared to be pushed down. I had always been taught to be a strong person and to fight for what was right. This suddenly took over. I had to fight and regain my high grades. I was going to show Chris that I wasn't a 'wimpish girl' and I was going to prove to myself that I could get back on top again.

So that is what I did. I began to work again in class. I pushed myself to complete just that little bit more in lessons. I took work home and spent my breaktimes catching up. Chris and his attitude made me work harder than I had ever done before. I was determined to prove him wrong. It wasn't long before people began to admire me. They all became aware of what I was doing and slowly they began to support me. Boys and girls were behind me giving me that extra push to work harder. It was just like before, the whole class pulling together as one.

To everyone's amazement Chris himself began to pay attention to me. He couldn't believe my accomplishment and slowly I won him over too. He stopped making chauvinistic comments and began to treat me with respect. I had done just what I set out to do — to prove him wrong, and whilst doing that I won his respect. Life got back to normal and I realised that the class had been drawn closer together as a result of this whole unpleasant episode. It was as if we had survived all the trouble and had pulled through together. Everyone had helped and we had made it. There was a sense of achievement in the atmosphere and in the end Chris had done some good and brought us all even closer.

Sheli Ullah (17)

The last year I spent in primary school was my most educational year, academically as well as socially. I learnt how to stand up for myself and not let others use me.

My class was made up of nineteen boys and eleven girls, all Bangladeshis except for the female teacher. Usually the boys would leave us alone, unless we provoked them. But at break-time the boys would start on girls to pass their time. Some boys would just start on girls to prove or to show off their masculinity to their friends, sometimes using very foul language. If the girls went to the teacher with a complaint then they would not be left alone until the boys got tired of the game.

Because of our cultural background, where it is important to keep the girls and boys separate, this is bred into our minds as soon as our sex is known at birth. There is no hostility between boys and girls, just a knowledge rooted deep in the mind which often presents itself unconsciously in our behaviour, even when not under the eyes of watchful parents. As girls, we should not talk to boys, or sit next to them. The older girls are almost jealously guarded.

When we had to do any group work in class then the groups would be mixed. The boys would be squashed on one side of the table with girls on the other side of the table. Some time in the middle of the year settings at tables for lunch changed. Before everyone had free choice to sit where they wanted to but after the new rules everyone had to sit three girls and three boys to a table. In classes the boys got best seats, first choice usually and a lot of attention from teachers. But there were a few aggressive girls in our class. We would give as good as the boys by not giving up without a fight. So we all got on reasonably well academically.

Socially I could not adjust to any kind of situation. At home I was the good docile daughter. But in school I would pretend to be the boy I never was but always wanted to be. Fighting at the slightest provocation, swearing like the boys and generally behaving as they did, but in dresses.

My biggest problem was insecurity. I do not know why. So I used to get very emotional after a fight, which I usually won as I used to be ruthless when I lost my temper. I would cry because I hurt the person too much. Now I can hide a lot of my feelings.

In time I developed this ability to avoid hearing anything that I did not like, pretending I did not hear or did not understand. None of my teachers noticed these things. My friends did, but they accepted me at face value without questioning my answers.

We let ourselves be exploited by the boys. The girls would not let themselves do what they wanted just because the boys fought dirty. With promises from the girls in my class backing me up, I would then in the middle of an argument find myself on my own with the girls backing up the boys. Because I am stubborn I find that I go on arguing on my own.

Haleema (15)

One aspect of equal opportunities I feel I am particularly aware of is racism. I am a fifteen-year-old Asian girl. I suppose I would actually be classified as coloured if I lived in South Africa, as my grandmother on my mother's side is Afro-caribbean, and her husband, Asian. My mother met my father when she came to England in 1969. My father had just arrived from Pakistan. They were married four years later.

I think, that because I am Asian, I am more aware of racism than a white person would be; for example, I feel that most insults such as 'Paki' are directed at me even if said to others.

I attended a fairly racially mixed Primary School, with roughly twenty-four to a class. None of the teachers were Black or Asian. We were never taught about racism, what it was and how hurtful it could be. I think if we had been maybe we would have understood what was going on around us, and wouldn't have done and said the things we did. Nevertheless the school tended to avoid the whole issue altogether, as if they were afraid to tackle it. Not that it was much of a problem, but it would have been good to know, instead of finding out the hard way, and hurting peoples' feelings.

The teachers were not racist at all, except for maybe one. There was an Asian boy in my class who tended to write very fast and very untidily. The teacher at the time constantly told him to slow down and concentrate more on the style and shape of his writing, but it was no use. Then one day the teacher exploded. 'No wonder you rush your writing so much, it's because you come from Russia!' Silence fell over the class and the boy in question lowered his head and pretended to be totally engrossed in his maths text book. The girl next to me turned to me and whispered 'that's racist isn't it?'. But I didn't know for sure.

In fact my best friend at the time (who was white) came up to me and told me she was racist. I didn't know then what it was, so I said nothing, she then told me her whole family was racist. I said nothing, what could I say? Looking back, I don't think she was racist otherwise I would not have been amongst her close friends. I think that maybe her parents, being racist, would have preferred her to mix only with other white children, so told her to mention it to me in the hope that I would stay away from her. I met her family once or twice and they did seem a little stiff and unfriendly. Even now if I see them they just give a little stiff nod or hello and then speed off.

Another incident I remember is when a new boy joined our class. He looked sort of Greekish and was very shy at first, and because he was new he got the usual flood of questions. 'What's your name?', 'Where do you come from?', 'Have you got a bike?'. He told us he was white but had a suntan; when a year has passed everyone began to suspect that this was not true. 'Why did you lie to us?', 'Why did you say you were white when you weren't?', 'So where's the bike?' I think he lied because he thought that if he was white he would have been treated better than if he had just said he came from Greece. But his skin colour didn't matter to us at all as we were a pretty mixed class. When we flooded him with the questions, he became very red and looked as if he were going to cry. I felt very sorry for him, and everyone just moved away not wanting to actually make him cry.

However his problems didn't end there. At play times the boy and girls would go off and separate themselves, the boys would play football and the girls bull-dog, skipping, ting-tang-tommy or He. Once in a while the boys would play with us as well but always about six of them, never just one. But the Greek boy would play with us more often than the other boys, and on his own as well. The other boys attacked him viciously calling him a 'girl' and a 'sissy'. He looked close to tears, but he just walked away from them and carried on playing with us. The other boys left him alone, and I think they secretly admired him for standing up to them, as they eventually allowed him to play with them. But from time to time he'd come back and play bull-dog with us.

Now that I am attending a secondary school they deal with issues like racism head on instead of pretending it doesn't exist. One of the first things we were told when joining the school was that they would not tolerate any form of racism, and they meant it! I think this is excellent as the school set the standards straight away and now there is little if any racism in the school.

Part II:
Classrooms and Curriculum

7 StoryBox

AMAR KHELA and MONICA DEB

Why is a child who speaks another European language in addition to English considered bright and interesting while a child bilingual in English and an Asian language is often seen as a potential educational problem? And why, in an educational system which has for so long prided itself on being child-centred, are the cultures and linguistic resources of some groups of pupils persistently ignored or disparaged? This chapter is about a project which was designed to value and celebrate the cultures and languages of all bilingual children, and to increase the awareness and understanding of monolingual and bilingual pupils about language diversity.

The Aims of StoryBox[1]

StoryBox grew from the belief that bilingualism is an asset to be valued, and not the hindrance to learning that earlier educationalists believed. Within Bradford, there is a wealth of languages, among which are Bengali, Chinese (Cantonese and Hakkar), English, Greek, Gujerati, Polish, Punjabi, Pushto and Urdu. But most of these languages, and the cultures with which they are associated, have not traditionally been valued, or celebrated, in school. In this chapter we want to show how the Story Box Project encouraged bilingual pupils to use a wide range of skills from all their languages, to become more confident about school work in general, and to grow in self esteem. The Project also worked towards increasing the awareness and understanding of all pupils involved, about language and language diversity. It supported teachers in developing new approaches to working across the curriculum.

The StoryBox Project celebrated multilingual skills through story making using a variety of media. The following points were central to our aims:

- A belief in the power of story making as a learning tool for all children but particularly to support and extend bilingual children.
- The importance of a cross curricular approach which opens up many possibilities for linking, sharing and developing ideas, skills and con-

cepts. The arts in particular can be an effective vehicle for children's academic and social development.

• The value of linking different age groups of pupils to work together. This empowers children to teach and learn from each other, and provides a purpose, setting and audience for their work.

• The need to explore and promote effective ways of facilitating access to the National Curriculum for all children. We particularly wanted to raise children's awareness of, and confidence in, their own skills by involving them in learning activities where they were the expert.

We wanted to create a climate of warmth and support in which self-confidence and self-esteem could grow and in which everyone felt valued and able to risk making mistakes. The emphasis was on building upon the interests and skills of teachers and artists which were then transmitted into giving choices to pupils. The approach was a fairly open ended one which allowed for the same task to be developed to different levels of achievement. Responses from pupils and teachers during the work would suggest that the Project provided many opportunities to counter racism, and to question ethnocentricism.

The Importance of Cross-phase Work

Arranging for older and younger pupils to work together was extremely important in order to achieve our aims. (Bradford has First Schools for children aged 5–9, Middle Schools for children aged 9–13, and Upper Schools for students aged 13–18.) Cross-phase work can lead children to become more aware of, and to value each other's skills and knowledge. As they teach and learn from each other, pupils become more confident in their own strengths and expertise, and develop a deeper understanding of each others' cultures.

Many Bradford Upper School bilingual students have not experienced the supportive language environment which first school pupils are now enjoying; they have not always had the opportunity to use their home language in the classroom. The enthusiasm and confidence of the younger children can provide these older students with a sufficiently relaxed environment to take risks in using languages other than English. Repeatedly in our work we were to find that younger pupils could provide the key to unlocking the older students' language potential. The older monolingual and bilingual students quickly recognised the advantages of learning bilingually, as they watched the younger children acquiring and developing concepts quickly and easily through using both their languages.

Mixed age groups can also provide real, purposeful and appreciative audiences for each other's work, and during the project we found that pupils became highly motivated to produce their very best, because of the strong personal relationships they were developing with older or younger children.

Planning the Work

We invited proposals from pairs of schools serving different age groups. Schools outlined the work they wanted to do, and undertook to supply five days supply cover for each of the two teachers who would act as co-ordinators. We also asked schools to identify a regular place on the timetable when cross-phase work would take place, including work with the artists. A commitment to regular meetings and the release of the school coordinater to collaborate with ourselves and the artists in planning, monitoring and evaluating the work, were vital to the success of the project.

On acceptance of a school's application they were asked to send a more detailed topic web for the work. This was followed by three days of INSET for artists and teachers. These were spent sharing skills, planning the work, and discussing how it could best be evaluated, by children, teachers and artists. Some of the artists had not worked in school before, and the INSET days were crucial for them, as well as for the teachers, in developing an awareness of the multilingual and cross-curricular nature of the project and of its educational aims.

We wanted the artists to be involved with teachers and pupils throughout the course of the work, rather than just appearing for a single session in school. We believed that if teachers, artists and children could plan, carry out and evaluate work together then the children would have more opportunity to express and develop a whole range of creative skills, and to produce really high quality work. In addition, teachers and artists could learn from each other's skills and experience.

The community artists we worked with were:

- Vayu, a story teller bilingual in English and Tamil.
- Adam and Tony, monolingual English story tellers who use masks and draw material from a wide variety of cultural traditions.
- Tyra, an Indian dancer bilingual in English and Urdu who encourages adults and children to develop their own movements from the basic steps of Indian dance.
- Lois and Jane, monolingual English-speaking shadow puppeteers, use a wide range of puppetry techniques, especially from the Far East.
- Andy, a monolingual English-speaking musician who uses rhythms and instruments from many different parts of the world.
- Buta and Attal, Urdu poets who are bilingual English and Urdu speakers.

The Work in School: Some Snapshots

After the initial three day planning session, the teachers and artists were well prepared to start work in school. Schools often agreed to designate one or two half days a week over one to two terms for the work, but the pattern varied. Artists worked in schools using a variety of media for multilingual storymaking — oral and written work, drama, puppetry, masks, music, dance, audio and video recordings. The worked covered a wide range of themes, for instance Earth and Space (involving English, art, science and humanities work), Food and Growth, Energy, the design of a playbus, a GCSE English project on story telling, and the Ramayana Story. The proportion of bilingual children in the schools involved varied from 20%– 100%, and we nearly always worked with whole classes containing a mixture of monolingual and bilingual pupils.

The playbus

One Upper School held a 'Cross Curricular Fortnight' each year, when the normal timetable was dropped and pupils could choose from a variety of projects. Some students chose the Story Box option to design and take a playbus to a nearby First School. They worked with Andy and teachers from the Drama, Home Economics, Language Support, Design and Technology departments to create a story, using puppets and a wide range of musical instruments. They made all their props and materials, and presented the performance to children in their linked first school, using the bus (the

windows made ideal screens for the shadow puppets!). The story explored ways of overcoming the barriers of language and communication through a character who spoke a language other than English.

Creating toys and stories

In another Upper School, students visited their linked First School every week, and worked in pairs with a small group of the younger children to design and make a toy, and to develop and write a story around it. The older children had been doing work on forces, and the younger children looking at different kinds of mechanical movement, including pulleys and friction. We ensured that the work would involve a strong language element through preparation with the pupils before the two different age-groups met. For instance, the older students carried out a simulation exercise where they pretended to be workers in a toy factory. All the 'overseers' were bilingual pupils, and English was not allowed to be spoken in the factory. We found this exercise useful in raising the awareness of all pupils about how restricted one is by not being able to use one's home language. As a result, students started to understand relationships between language and power.

The 'journey through life'

A more detailed look at a third example shows how building on children's existing skills and experiences enhances their self esteem and confidence through feeling that their languages and cultures are valued and recognised by the school. It also shows how pupils were encouraged to recognise and appreciate everyone's achievements, great and small.

A class of seven to nine-year-olds from a first school which was almost 100% bilingual was linked with a class of fourteen-year-olds in an upper school which contained a mixture of monolingual and bilingual students. They worked together on a project entitled 'Journey Through Life'. This project focused on children's personal stories, stories based on incidents from their past where their own histories, cultures and backgrounds were of significance. Each pupil was asked to think of three important events in their life so far and bring from home items which symbolised these events. Children shared their stories with each other in languages of their choice. It was with pride and pleasure that they shared their items, explaining the significance of the things they had brought in. One of Shabana's items was a beautiful bracelet which she had received from her family on completing her reading of the Quran. Jasbir brought his first kara (bracelet) he had worn as a small child and Anita brought in a rattle which she had as a baby.

Having shared their stories and shown their items the pupils worked together with their teachers and Adam, Tyra, Butta and Attal to create imaginative pieces of work portraying their events symbolically and using a variety of media including paints, dance, masks, music and poetry.

   This work involved children using their own language expertise, for example, Shomsun, a keen and highly motivated seven-year-old had newly arrived from Bangladesh. She had good literacy skills in Bengali but understood hardly any English. She was very much admired by her peers for her Bengali skills and was constantly asked for words in Bengali. She volunteered to make a Bengali dictionary with illustrations for class use. The teacher suggested that the dictionary be based on the items that the pupils had brought in. Shomsun had to arrange the words in alphabetical order. With support from her peers, she learned the words in English and then made an English to Bengali dictionary which was also arranged in alphabetical order. These dictionaries became a constant source of reference for younger and older pupils as well as for the teachers and artists. Meanwhile, without being asked, other children offered Shamsun support and translation, in English. Her bilingual teacher encouraged her to do written work in Bengali, and then translated it with her into English. As one teacher wrote: 'Creating space for pupils to use their bilingual skills gives them opportunity to demonstrate their expertise.'

   The artists also were adventurous in their use of language. The surprise and delight on the pupils' faces is unforgettable as Adam, a monolingual English-speaking artist, opened up a workshop by singing a Bengali song. This demonstrated to the children the value that he attached to the language. It also inspired the usually reluctant bilingual children to volunteer words and phrases in languages other than English. He had also learnt words in Hinko, Pushto, Punjabi and Urdu which undoubtedly gained him respect from the pupils. As Adam put it: 'We have to find the courage to step into the richness of multilingualism'.

   A genuine sharing of skills took place between the older and younger pupils throughout the project and was particularly highlighted during the mask-making sessions. The younger pupils had spent a considerable amount of time investigating materials in relation to planning, and making models of the items they had brought in to school. When making masks together, it was with confidence and clarity that they informed the older pupils of what they had learned. They advised their older partners about which glue was appropriate and about strengthening and joining techniques. The older students were impressed and encouraged the younger children to share and demonstrate what they had discovered. One older student said, 'Working with younger children helped me gain confidence. I've become a responsible person. I'm more mature about life in general ... both inside and outside school'. Another wrote 'children are like adults, they're only smaller ... they've got lots of ideas'.

After taking part in the 'Journeys Through Life' workshops, the younger pupils were able to pass on the skills they had developed to other children in their own First School. They became workshop facilitators for these children, after having discussed what they themselves had learnt, and how they could best communicate it to others. They shared stories which had been created with other classes in storymaking sessions. In one group Zia who was hard of hearing was too shy to tell his story in front of a group. The rest of his group suggested he put his story on to tape to support a mime piece they could create for their workshop group. With encouragement and support from his peers he did this and glowed with pride when his tape was played to other children.

Evaluation

Evaluation was an integral part of the whole process. Regular evaluation and planning sessions took place with pupils, as well as separate ones with teachers and artists. This promoted a clear sense of direction and ownership. At the end of every session, children were always given some time to reflect on what had been achieved, and to plan what should be done next. Sometimes this was more formal, as in the evaluation sheet below, completed by older and younger children working together. We designed this in a way

THE STORY BOX PROJECT - Week 3

Name . . . .

Work in pairs or small groups (with children from both schools). Talk about the questions. Put everybody's ideas down on paper - even if you don't all agree. Don't miss anything out! Take it in turns to write.

1. What are the things you have enjoyed most about the project so far?

2. How do you feel about using languages other than English?

3. How do you feel about standing up and performing in front of other children?

4. What's it like working with younger or older children?

5. Is there anything we could do to make the project even better?

which we hoped would convey the respect and value we had for pupils' own experience and feelings, and would help them to focus on positive achievements. The exercise encouraged pupils to talk about, and consolidate their work, bringing groups closer together and developing individual children's confidence. It also provided valuable information which could be included in pupils' records of achievement, as well as for the artists, and ourselves.

Younger children filled in the following evaluation sheets and then discussed the areas of work they found difficult with their teacher.

Name : _____

Please circle any of the following you found difficult doing :

working with others

meeting new people   playing music

                                                                                          drama

listening   joining in

                                                                        dancing

talking in front of others

                                        speaking in my language

          singing

                                                    sharing my ideas

          taking photos   being with my partner

What else did you find difficult ?

Name: _____

Please circle the things you did well.

I worked in groups

        I listened to others

I shared my ideas with adults

        I made some good decisions

I solved problems

        I behaved sensibly

I tried hard.

        I took part.

        I shared my ideas with my group

I worked with my partner

What else did you do well?

In one school children designed their own evaluation sheets and translated them into other languages; the evaluation sheet on p. 87 was translated into Urdu, and written out in both Urdu and Roman script (see pp. 88 and 89). The Roman script was for those childrem who could speak Urdu but who had not learnt the Arabic script.

We wanted pupils to use what they learnt from this kind of evaluation in planning their own future work. For instance, the Upper School students who worked with younger children to design a toy and then create a story around it had a number of preparatory sessions on story making before visiting the First School. They were asked at the end of one session to consider how far they felt its aims had been achieved and then use this discussion to help their own planning of the story-making session which they themselves would lead, with a group of younger children.

As well as involving children in the ongoing evaluation, it was important for teachers and artists to have some time out of the classroom to reflect on how the work was going. We had one Inset day about half way through the work for reviewing and planning, and a day at the end of the work to carry out an overall evaluation, and discuss longer term implications.

STORY BOX

NAme _____
CLASS _____
SCHOOL _____
GrouP _____

WhAT did You do
_____
_____

Who did You woRK witH

Which thing did you Like.
_____

WhAT thingS didnt You Like
_____

DiD You MAKe some New FREnds
Who Were thAy

designed by IWas NASir Grosvenor 1st School.

In their overall evaluations of work with the project, teachers wrote with satisfaction and occasional astonishment about the achievements of their bilingual pupils. Monolingual teachers had gained confidence in supporting bilingual children's language development. And they felt children from all language backgrounds had benefited from the cross-age, cross-curricular approach. Some schools experienced problems in finding the time needed for planning, and the organisation involved in getting children from one school to another was always demanding. The benefits of working intensively with a small group of pupils had to be balanced against the desire to offer experience of StoryBox activities to as many children as possible. In

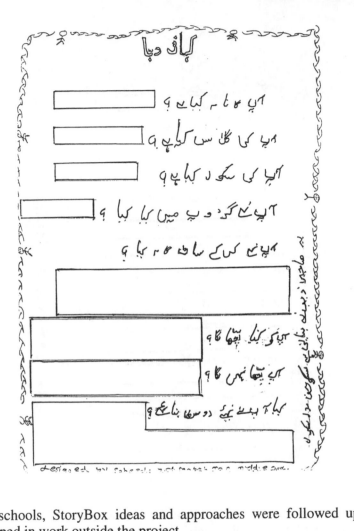

some schools, StoryBox ideas and approaches were followed up and developed in work outside the project.

After the Project

The funding for StoryBox has officially ended, but many of the people involved are finding ways of carrying on the work they developed over the last four years. Teachers and artists, as well as children, have acquired new skills and enthusiasms. Teachers are continuing to use the artistic skills they learnt in the Project, e.g. producing videos, making shadow puppets. Adam now has his own freelance company offering schools a contract with clear aims and objectives, story-making projects which involve a strong multi-

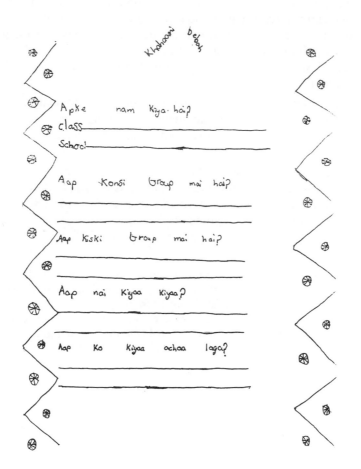

lingual focus and ongoing inbuilt evaluation. For some schools the issues raised by StoryBox provided the starting point for work on a language policy; in others they helped towards establishing cross curricular methods, and new ways of approaching language work. Many teachers found it a revelation to see how previously unmotivated and sometimes disruptive pupils responded to work where their own language and culture were recognised and valued. Others have incorporated regular evaluation sessions with pupils into their work.

All of the work that took place was underpinned by a commitment to equal opportunities, and to anti-racism. The StoryBox approach valued the skills and knowledge of everyone involved: pupils and teachers. The open-ended nature of activities provided opportunities for all abilities to participate and to have a sense of achievement. Children worked from their own strengths and creativity which cut across divisions and inequalities created by the English language based curriculum. Our methods of evaluation were designed to increase the confidence of pupils from all backgrounds and all levels of ability.

The StoryBox Project approach promoted interpersonal relationship which transcended divisions of language and culture and helped pupils to understand and value their own experiences and achievements and those of others.

In our posts as Advisory Teachers we continue to support and promote ways of working which ensure equality of access for all children. Everyone has a tale to tell and as a seven-year-old once exclaimed 'Take me Miss, I'm full of stories bursting to come out!'.

Notes

1. From 1986 to 1990 StoryBox was sponsored jointly by the Bradford Educational Authority and the Department of Teaching Studies at Bradford and Ilkley Community College with financial support from Yorkshire Arts for community artist residencies in schools. Teachers were encouraged to evaluate part of the work in which they were involved, and could use this towards gaining an award in the West Yorkshire Inset Accreditation Scheme.

8 Global Education for Equality

MARGOT BROWN

Margot Brown's chapter on global education discusses the importance of the processes as well as the content of an equal opportunities curriculum, particularly for ethnic minority pupils and girls. She suggests that equality education has three aspects: education about equality, for equality and in equality. None of these can stand alone. Children can develop their critical faculties through the strategies of global education, develop their self esteem, their ability to value others and work collaboratively. The chapter concludes with a practical project for putting these ideals into action.

Introduction

Global education deals with the concepts of equality and inequality, power and lack of power and interdependence. In this chapter I will explore how global education can contribute to children's understanding and knowledge about equality issues. Although they interact and are mutually supportive, I will distinguish between three aspects of global education, namely education *about* equality, education *for* equality, and education *in* equality.

Education About Equality

Extending and developing children's perspectives

'Some children were inspired by work on an environment project to keep the playground tidy and litter-free. One playtime they approached the headteacher who was on playground duty:

"Look, we've collected 30 bits of rubbish".

"Well done!" responds the head. "The playground looks much better now."

Imagine his feelings a few moments later when the same children are seen feeding the rubbish through the railings of the playground, into the street beyond.'

Stories like this encourage people to believe that children's understanding and world view is limited by their immediate environment and experience. The danger is then that they do not attempt to take the starting points for child-centred work any further. Many children in British primary classrooms know quite a lot about the wider world through their everyday experience of family, friends and language, though this is not always recognised and drawn upon in school. Furthermore, children growing up in our rapidly changing multi-ethnic, multilingual and often confusing society are bombarded with information. Advertising hoardings, books, cartoons and comics, television and toy catalogues all contribute to children's developing views. These sources reflect many perspectives and children need help to understand them.

Global education offers a framework for making sense of the world at personal, local, national and global levels. At the heart of this framework is recognising connections. Our individual decisions and cumulative actions are affected by and can also affect people thousands of miles away. Topics like 'The world in a supermarket bag' and 'What is our classroom made of?' explore the trade connections in the clothes we wear, the food we eat, the machines we drive or use in the home. Such work makes explicit the interdependence of our lives as consumers with the lives of producers, and highlights some of the inequalities inherent in relationships between countries in the more powerful northern hemisphere, and those in the South.

Many British links between countries and peoples have their roots in colonialism and are impossible to understand without a historical perspective, acknowledging for example, the debt owed by the Industrial Revolution to the profits of slavery. Examining interdependence without reference to inequalities in the relationships and the causes of those inequalities, disguises and distorts the reality. This is true of relationships at all levels, between North and South, between countries or, at a personal level, between people.

It is not common for schools to analyse or make explicit the power relations and perspectives in their selection of topics. We regularly present pupils with a male, white, European and middle class view of the world. As an example, 1992 marked the quincentenary of Christopher Columbus' voyage to the lands which became known as the Americas. This historical event features regularly in the school curriculum and is included in the English statutory orders for history — but from whose perspective? Are the voices of the indigenous people heard? Is there a true recognition of the complexity of the original societies, their history, languages and traditions? Whose knowledge is valued and presented to students? Are certain actions justified by dehumanising one group of people at the expense of another?

A curriculum project about equality: Native Americans

In primary schools the familiar project of North American Indians (now usually referred to as Native Americans) regularly exhibits just this bias and distortion. The lives of North American Indians are presented to children locked in a time warp. The curriculum approach seldom indicates that they are alive today doing a variety of jobs and with hopes, fears and emotions related to their contemporary lives. Their struggle for land rights, against prejudice and discrimination and to maintain traditional values is not usually part of the topic. Yet the National Curriculum Council guidance document 8 (Education for Citizenship 1990) argues that issues of rights and responsibilities concern us all and should be part of the curriculum.

Another consequence of focusing on 'braves', war and heroic male deeds is to render women and children invisible. Native American women are presented as shadowy figures tending children, moving in and out of tepees and generally servicing the 'braves'. Learning about women chiefs such as Chouteau Rosana Musgrove, or Wetamoo is conspicuous by its absence. There are opportunities here to challenge — or reinforce — male/female stereotypes as well as racial ones, but these depend on teachers raising questions about power and how some knowledge is privileged.

Concepts of equality and justice may seem hard enough without the added problem of exploring them through the experience of indigenous peoples. Yet this is a very rich approach, for children can become aware of different value systems and start to grapple with the complexities of rights and responsibilities, of stereotyping and majority attitudes to minorities — global issues which affect us all wherever we live.

Given the will to do so, how can teachers find the resources to question the myths created by decades of Hollywood films (with a few notable exceptions), comics and storybooks which have consistently portrayed Native Americans as the enemy — and a savage one at that? The Council on Interracial Books for Children has produced a pack entitled 'Unlearning Indian stereotypes' which consists of tape, filmstrip (readily converted to slides) and teachers' booklet of information and teaching ideas. A teacher of 9–10 year-olds in Ealing used the suggestions in the booklet, and supplemented them with other material. She began by asking her class to draw a Native American and the house that the person lived in. No one asked if she meant in the past or present. Almost all the class drew a man, dressed in feathers and leather, standing outside a tepee. She then asked the class to mark the particular features on their drawings which identified the person as Indian. Later class discussion exposed the stereotypes, myths and assumptions that these children — themselves from several different cultural/ethnic backgrounds — held about Native Americans.

She then showed the children the slide/tape presentation. This is a documentary in which the main characters are young people from various Indian nations. Each gives information about clothes, homes and traditional work in their own nation, but also talks about their feelings at being misrepresented in children's story books. The children were encouraged to be critical of their initial assumptions that Native Americans are an homogeneous group and the class developed considerable empathy with the young Native Americans in the slide/tape. They began to identify, collect and analyse the representation of Native Americans in comics, cartoons and other less likely sources such as birthday cards and alphabet friezes. They broadened their discussions, for example through considering how other groups in our society are also stereotyped.

The teacher decided to build on these beginnings through exploring the feelings of Native Americans with respect to the Settlers; she read the class extracts from *We Are Mesquakie, We Are One* by Hadley Irwin. One section made a particular impact. The central character of the book, a young Mesquakie woman named Hidden Doe, has to go to school to learn English:

'We sat on benches made of wood, hard and polished like stones washed often by the rain. We were in rows like planted corn and not in circles. We were not to move.

Gray Gull taught but one. White Teacher taught many.

White Teacher was strange. His eyes were pale, like the sky when clouds hide the colour. His hair was yellow like wild mustard. His lips were thin and opened like the carp when it lies upon the river bank, snared by a spear.

He held up the White Ones' flag and said, "A-mer-i-ca, A-mer-i-ca".

We repeated, "A-mer-i-ca, A-mer-i-ca".

Then he pointed at each of us and said, "A-mer-i-can", and each one said it after him.

He pointed to me, "A-mer-i-can. A-mer-i-can".

'Mes-quak-ie', I said.

We did this many times until he became very red and then he decided to name stones.

He placed the stones in a row on the platform, and as he set them down he called them, "One, Two, Three, Four, Five".

He did it again and again and the others repeated his words. He pointed to each and each said the words. He pointed to me. I did not speak. Why would I name stones? I could grow old and blind naming just the stones in Stony Creek.

I sat on a high stool in a corner the rest of the day. Everyone could see that I was Mesquakie.

I learned other words that day: uncivilised, papoose, squaw. They were not pretty words.

I spoke to my father, Great Bear. "I can go no more to White Ones' school. Though we must starve, I cannot go. Un-civ-il-ised. '"(pp. 56–57)

This extract raised issues about language and power and the children started to consider a variety of probing questions: whose rights and whose needs were served in the excerpt about going to school? Why are Native Americans called by the insulting term 'Red Indians'? Whose perspective are we taking when we talk about 'the New World' or 'the discovery of America'?

Thus far the class had not thought in any depth about contemporary Native Americans. They now read *Red Ribbons for Emma*. This story is about the struggle for land in which many Native Americans are currently involved. Emma challenges stereotypes about Native Americans typical of

Red Ribbons for Emma

children's books. She is a woman with a name and a nation — Navajo. She
has a job, as a shepherd and an office cleaner. She is a grandmother.

'Emma is brave and strong and courageous. And she is not alone. Many
of her people work and struggle with her. They are brave, strong, and
courageous heroes, too. They are the rural Navajo people. They call
themselves 'grassroots' people because, like the hardy grass on their
reservation, they have to be tough to survive. Grassroots means that
like the grass, they have their roots in the land.'

'Emma and the other rural Navajos look different from heroes we
usually read about who are mostly men, mostly white men. Emma is a
poor Indian woman and a grandmother. She is friendly and fun to be
with.' (*Red Ribbons for Emma*: p. 5)

The story is about Emma's struggle to keep the land for her sheep against
the encroachment of a coal mining company supplying a power plant built
on Navajo land. The book raises issues of *power, rights and responsibilities*:
not only of land rights and treaty observance but also of pollution and
environmental damage caused by the mining companies. These are issues
which connect us across national boundaries.

Education for Equality

Empowering children and developing self esteem and collaboration

Global education is also concerned with empowering children themselves through developing self esteem and the ability to communicate and
collaborate. There are a variety of activities which help children deal with
negative feelings in positive and supportive ways, and to learn skills for
peaceful conflict resolution. In part this means affirming the children's
community and personal background and developing awareness about
gender, 'race', class and language.

However, there is little point in cooperative work or affirmation activities
within the classroom if inequalities in society are ignored. Words like
'respect' and 'tolerance' feature frequently in discussions about equality.
While acknowledging the goodwill and positive intent I confess to having
problems with both these words in this context. In its definition of 'respect'
the Collins English Dictionary includes 'deference', 'admiration' and 'esteem for'. Defining respect in this way can support conservative and even
reactionary attitudes about appropriate roles and behaviour for women and
girls and a teacher strongly committed to equality and justice could be put
in a highly ambiguous position. The term 'tolerance' also has overtones of
'put up with' or 'allow or permit to exist' which sit uneasily with notions
of equality. Equality is more than tolerance and respect. What if a group is

behaving in an intolerant or oppressive way? The message is that we must be very clear about our own values and priorities and sensitive to our own prejudices, but acknowledge that working towards equality may mean recognising conflicting power bases and challenging the status quo.

Education for equality is concerned with the skills which children need to work productively and collaboratively. These are the dynamic, overt teaching strategies of global education, namely interactive group work which encourages children to work together, share and respond to each other's views. The skills they will need to develop are not just those of successful collaboration — that is, the ability to ask questions, listen and contribute to group work — but also critical abilities, to detect bias and omissions in resources, and to analyse and understand different perspectives. There is not space to go into detail here, but I recommend activities in the resources list at the end of this chapter.

Education in Equality

Where education for equality is concerned with the processes through which children learn, education in equality is about the context of their learning, the messages they 'absorb through their pores'. Children cannot develop high self esteem and respect for others' views in one part of the curriculum if the ethos and environment of the school is giving contradictory messages.

A Project which Contributes to all Three Aspects of Equality Work

In the next few paragraphs I will describe a teacher's work with 9–11 year-old children in Kirkless Education Authority, as part of a Diploma in Global and Multicultural Education. The project reveals how the three strands of education about, for and in equality weave together and support one another.

Elizabeth Moody worked in a school in a village on the outskirts of a northern town. Twenty per cent of the class were Muslim children of Pakistani origin. The majority of the class were from low income backgrounds. She planned work which focused particularly on gender issues, but met immediately with violent resistance from a core of boys in the class. Moreover, she commented that 'collaborative learning was an alien concept to them. They only worked individually or in competition with each other. Their fear of failure was so strong that they would not even try to answer questions ...' Hostility to the offered content and issues of self-esteem and self worth could not be separated from the processes of the class project.

Children who are unsure and unwilling to reveal their own views often remain silent or go to the other extreme and dominate conversation. In some cases they set out deliberately to disrupt. The more sensitive the issues, and therefore for some children the more threatening, the more it is essential to build up real confidence and interactive skills including an understanding of when to speak and when to be silent.

In order to build up an atmosphere of confidence and receptiveness to new ideas and new ways of working, Elizabeth introduced work on turn taking, listening and reporting back. Some of these activities were carried out in a circle, some in pairs or small groups. Exercises in talking and listening skills were designed to break down barriers of resistance and build up children's ability and confidence to take turns in debate, express points of view clearly and rationally and develop the all important skills of listening. One such exercise is 'magic microphone'. Anything can substitute for a real microphone, for instance a shell or a stone. This is passed round a circle of children and only the child holding the 'magic microphone' may speak. When their turn is over, the child passes the microphone on to the next person. No one is forced to speak, and may pass it on without comment. Other activities of this sort are described in Fisher & Hicks (1985).

The project itself began from the children's own experience and focused on 'family'. An initial activity looked at the distribution of work in the family, through 'tools about the house' (described in *Gender Activities*, Susan Fountain, 1990). In small groups, children explored the concept of 'skill' and its relationship to work and gender in the home. They made lists of the various tools used to keep the home functioning, who usually used them and how much skill was involved. They also had to consider how often the tool was used, whether daily, weekly, monthly or annually. There was some anger as the survey revealed that essential and regularly used tools such as mops or the cooker, were mainly the preserve of women and girls. Some boys claimed that men had to do all the heavy work but the girls pointed out that carrying wet washing, a baby or shopping was also heavy work.

The children suggested a test to sort out the argument. When parents came to pick up their children from the school nursery, all infants and toddlers who could not walk a stipulated distance were weighed. The range was 11kg–18kg. That same afternoon each pupil in the class walked twice round the football field carrying a 'baby' made from a sack of sand. It may not have been the same as carrying a squirming, lively toddler but assumptions about heavy work and the weaker sex were certainly revised!

Elizabeth now invited a number of women and men into the school, all of whom worked in non-stereotypical jobs, for the children to meet and interview. The class continued to reassess things they had previously taken for granted as 'normal' and to consider what was open to change. In this project the processes and the content were both designed to promote equality and challenge assumptions and expectations about traditional gender roles.

Conclusions

In the reality of the classroom, education about, for and in equality cannot be separated.

Education about equality — the equality 'content' — requires that time be allocated within the curriculum to learn from the experience of people in their own community past or present, be they civil rights workers, suffragettes or anti-slavers from within and outside the slave community. In addition to the sources mentioned already, resources such as *Underground to Canada* (Smucker, 1978) or *Roll of Thunder, Hear my Cry* (Taylor, 1980) can provide the material that children work on, helping to undermine stereotypes and widen their knowledge and understanding.

Education for equality means developing skills such as critical analysis, detecting omissions, building relationships and understanding different perspectives, listening and asking relevant questions, communication and negotiation. Education about and for equality are the knowledge and skills of the curriculum.

Education in equality acknowledges the importance of children's sense of self worth, ability to respect others' views and develop a value system based on fairness and justice. It implies consistent messages and a positive ethos in the classroom and in the school.

Together the three are the contribution of global education to a more just world.

Acknowledgement

I am grateful to Elizabeth Moody for allowing me to draw on her work.

References

The Council on Interracial books for Children (1977) *Unlearning 'Indian' Stereotypes: A Teaching Unit*. 1841 Broadway, New York NY 10023, USA.
Fisher, S. and Hicks, D. (1985) What is a classroom made of? *World Studies 8-13, A Teacher's Handbook*. Edinburgh: Oliver & Boyd.

Irwin, H. (1984) *We Are Mesquakie, We Are One*. London: Sheba Feminist Publishers.
Oxfam (1987) *The World in a Supermarket Bag*. Oxfam Education, 274 Banbury Road, Oxford.
Fountain, S. (1991) *Gender Issues: An Activity File*. Somerset: Stanley Thornes.
National Curriculum Council (1990) *Curriculum Guidance and Education for Citizenship*.
New Mexico People and Energy Collective (1981) *Red Ribbons for Emma*. New Seed Press, PO Box 3016, Stanford CA 94305, USA.
Smucker, B. (1978) *Underground to Canada*. Harmondsworth: Puffin, Penguin Press.
Taylor, M. (1980) *Roll of Thunder, Hear my Cry*. Harmondsworth: Puffin, Penguin Press.
Taylor, M. (1982) *Let the Circle be Unbroken*. London: Gollancz.

Resources for global education

Fountain, S. (1990) *Learning Together, Global Education 4–7*. Somerset: Stanley Thornes.
Hicks, D. and Steiner, M. (1989) *Making Global Connections: A Teacher's Workbook*. Edinburgh: Oliver and Boyd.
Hicks, D. W. (1981) *Minorities: A Teacher's Resource Book for the Multi Ethnic Curriculum*. London: Heinemann Education Books.
McFarlane, C. (1986) *Hidden Messages: Activities for Exploring Bias*. Birmingham: Development Education Centre.
Pike, G. and Selby, D. (1988) *Global Teacher, Global Learner*. London: Hodder & Stoughton.
Preiswerk, R. (ed.) (1981) *The Slant of the Pen: Racism in Children's Books*. Geneva: World Council of Churches.

Photopacks

Photographs are a useful tool for teachers planning cooperative tasks. They also allow children to develop skills of visual literacy. The skills can help children:

- understand and challenge stereotypes
- ask questions
- develop critical thinking
- gain information
- recognise messages
- clarify values.

From Birmingham Development Education Centre, Gillett Centre, Selly Oak Colleges, Bristol Road, Birmingham:

- *Working Now* — photographs and activities for exploring gender roles in the primary classroom.

- *Behind the Scenes* — photographs and in-service activities for exploring the hidden curriculum.
- *Us and the Kids* — ideas and resources for parent groups.
- *What is a Family?* — photographs and activities.
- *New Journeys* — Teaching about other places: Learning from Kenya and Tanzania.

From Centre for World Development Education, Regent's College, Inner Circle, Regent's Park, London NW1 4NS:

- *Pictures of Health in a Changing World.*

From Greenlight Publications, Ty Bryn, Llangynog, Carmarthen: Dyfed.

- *Working Together* — exploring values in education.

From Invicta Book Service, 162 Coppice Street, Oldham, Lancashire OL8 4BJ:

- *Emotions* — pack of ten A4 black and white photographs.
- *Playground Games* — pack of ten A4 black and white photographs.

From Leeds Development Education Centre, 151 Cardigan Road, Leeds LS6 1LJ:

- *Disasters in the Classroom* — teaching about disasters in the Third World.

From Save the Children Fund, Mary Datchelor House, 17 Grove Lane, London SE5 8RD:

- *Homes* — photographs and teaching ideas about homes and housing issues around the world.

From Trentham Books, Unit 13/14 Trent Trading Park, Botteslow Street, Stoke-on-Trent:

- *Doing Things* — in and about the home.

From Oxfam Education, 274 Banbury Road, Oxford:

- *Photo Opportunities* — pack of colour photographs from Oxfam diaries to encourage children to examine and analyse photographs as evidence.

From Minority Rights Group, 379 Brixton Road, London SW9 7DE:

- *We Have Always Lived Here: The Maya of Guatemala* by Margaret Burr, edited by Rachel Warner. An active learning pack for Key Steps 2 and 3.

9 Some Equality Issues in Primary Design and Technology

ANNE WALDON

At the time of writing, a review of technology in the national curriculum is taking place, one of whose terms of reference highlights a requirement 'to ensure that the technical skills, knowledge and understanding of pupils at all stages are developed through work with and in relation to construction materials and related components and systems.' The review is part of an ongoing debate on the technology curriculum — one that is likely to continue over the next year or so. Anne Waldon's chapter, focusing on the current technology curriculum and written some time before the present revision, offers another perspective on this debate. Anne writes from a feminist standpoint which values female contributions and approaches to design and technology. She acknowledges the value of positive action to equip females to cope better in a male defined world, but asks how it has come about that women and minority groups have been marginalised and deskilled in design and technology, and now are perceived as needing induction by a skilled male elite. She argues that the current attainment targets in the national curriculum Design and Technology are actually the blueprint for radically rethinking the old male centred technology. However, this will only happen if teachers critically review the traditional CDT stance and recognise the centrality of the people who need, use and benefit from technological solutions, and value person-centred rather than machine-centred approaches.

This chapter looks at the 'new' subject, Design and Technology, which, along with Information Technology, was introduced under the Education Reform Act, 1988. It explores some of the differences between the broader view embodied in the 1990 National Curriculum documents and the older 'primary CDT' approach, showing the limitations of the old view, and suggesting that the new view offers far more powerful learning experiences for children, in which equal opportunities are embedded into the nature of the subject. In the initial section I look at the limitations of everyday concepts of technology, and talk very briefly about the history of education in this area. I will then discuss the range and potential of the National Curriculum requirements, and present a short case study which illustrates some of the equal opportunities aspects of Design and Technology within the classroom.

Defining 'Technology': Inside and Outside Schools

In the world outside education, and to most people within it, the word technology conjures up certain kinds of images: people usually think of computers, machines of various kinds, complicated and 'difficult' objects. Television programmes and other media talk of 'new technology', which will 'revolutionise' health care or transport or energy production. Few people, especially women, feel confident and competent in these areas. Views on appropriate jobs and behaviour for women and men have often resulted in women being steered towards 'soft' and caring work concerned with people; they may be expected to operate aspects of 'new technology', for example, to use word processors and X-ray scanners, but not to invent, order, install or repair them. The people who will be doing these sorts of things are assumed to be men, and this split has been reflected in the educational opportunities traditionally offered to each sex.

Meanwhile, the everyday idea of technology also carries with it a sense of progress, development and often desirability. New machines and techniques are generally considered 'a good thing', as programmes like *Tomorrow's World* illustrate. Industrialisation and the development of new technology are measures of the status of countries within the world community. Poorer, less 'developed' countries in technological terms, tend to be assumed to be poorer all round, culturally, socially, and morally.

These assumptions are easily made because much discussion of technology focuses on the machines themselves, and not on the way they are used, or affect and alter people's lives and feelings. This emphasis on machines obscures the fact that they are there to fulfil human purposes: medical technology claims to improve people's health, computers are used to save time and provide a better service to people, machines make things that people need and want.

This linking of machines with solutions to the technological problems is both part of and also perpetuates gender, class and 'race' divisions in power and decision-making. For example, people entering technologically-related jobs and careers find themselves separated out along these lines, becoming machine operators, maintenance engineers, designers or decision-makers accordingly. Access to the higher echelons is restricted via education and training requirements, which not only produces a small elite (in this country, mainly white, middle-class males), but also in the process reinforces its 'high tech', high prestige assumptions.

Since society in general shares these assumptions, such people have disproportionate power to decide what 'problems' technology should address. In any particular situation, different groups will identify different problems, will prefer different outcomes, and would probably choose different ways of tackling the difficulties. Yet whatever action or inaction is finally chosen will affect them all. The difficulty here is that access to the power to define the technological problem is very limited — women, ethnic minorities, children, all disadvantaged groups, find it difficult to have their views of problems recognised, despite having to live with the consequences of actions taken by those with more power.

An example is the problem of traffic congestion. The problem, as defined by car users and the road lobby, is clearly about the difficulties of getting through cities reasonably quickly. This makes considerable sense from their perspective, and more and better roads become an obvious solution. This kind of thinking has been characterised as the 'technological fix': high status technological solutions to the problems identified by high status groups. The difficulty is that it fails to consider the needs and wants of other groups affected by the situation, for example, people without access to cars, people with physical disabilities, those living near heavily-used roads, transport workers, people for whom resources are not available because they have been used to support the production of cars, lorries and roads, and those affected by pollution. There is a further complication in that some people may belong to more than one interest group, for instance suffering from the noise and pollution of a busy main road, but also contributing to it by using a car themselves.

School education in technology has always reflected conventional views. There has been a long tradition of preparing less academic boys for apprenticeships through practical 'making' skills in metal and wood, and preparing girls to be wives and mothers. These skills-focused curricula have strongly influenced their modern successors, courses such as CDT and Home Economics, which despite an increasing emphasis on people-focused problem solving and considering the implications of applying technology, have syllabuses rooted in the original intentions for the subjects. With their insistence on large bodies of knowledge and training in technical 'making' skills, these courses have offered teachers little scope for challenging a machine-centred view of technology.

Until recently developments in technological education in primary schools have mostly been based on secondary school models. 'Primary CDT', supported by trainers and teaching materials from the secondary (and largely male) CDT tradition, has focused on making things work and learning about tools and materials. Female teachers and pupils have been identified as lacking the appropriate skills and knowledge. Now, rather confusingly, national curriculum design and technology has been introduced: a new subject, with almost the same name but a radically different view of the purposes of technological education, which takes into account the critique of technology outlined above.

Design and Technology in the National Curriculum

Gender barriers in work and society have shifted a little, giving wider choice to individuals; the interdependence of the countries of the world in both environmental and economic terms is becoming clearer. For the future we need people who can assess the relevance and impact of technology as well as implement their own ideas. Education is one forum for tackling the structural inequalities operating in technology. In particular it is clear that there is no neutral way of teaching technology. Continuing to work in the traditional way maintains the status quo, and the inequality of opportunity already existing.

National curriculum design and technology works in a different, wider field from the old technology. Its clear overall purpose is to give individuals the capability to improve and develop the made world. This new aim has enormous implications for which the simple acquisition of technical skills to produce objects is not sufficient. Children are now required to question and evaluate solutions to identified problems, to consider how they benefit or disadvantage particular people, to imagine different, better possibilities and how changes might produce unexpected outcomes.

The four design and technology Attainment Targets provide a 'potted' version of these ideas. Target 1 addresses the problem of who decides what the problem ('need or opportunity') is. It transfers the responsibility for this from the teacher to the children, paralleling a possible wider political change. The children should explore and express not only their own views of a situation ('context'), but also those of other people, through interviews, discussion and research, and decide between conflicting interests in order to define the need or opportunity as they see it. Part of the teacher's role is to ensure that there is real equality of opportunity in this process, by ensuring, for example, that all the children have a say, and that the views expressed by other people in the research process are taken into account in the children's discussions.

Target 2 requires children to focus on the characteristics that any proposal will need to have in order to meet identified needs and opportunities (the performance specification), and to evaluate the ideas and possibilities they generate. Teachers can use this to develop the children's imaginative and speculative thinking, 'What is your design intended to do?' 'What must it never do?' 'What would happen if you chose that idea?' 'Which idea would be best from so-and-so's point of view?' Again equality of opportunity lies in the genuine exploration of different viewpoints.

Target 3 covers the development of the children's skills in implementing their ideas ('making'). The phrase 'artefacts, systems and environments' refers to the range of possible outcomes of design and technology, and offers one way of checking for balance: over a period of time, each child should develop outcomes across this range. Teacher intervention may be needed, since there is evidence that girls often prefer system and environmental solutions where people work together to make things happen, and boys prefer to produce artefacts, where the focus is on the working of things. Many texts and resources interpret 'systems' substantially as sets of objects working to perform a task, for example, the components of a bicycle. This is a much narrower view than that of the NC document which also emphasises processes and activities performed by people. Women and girls are often skilled in the development and fine-tuning of process solutions to difficulties, and to undervalue this marginalises a female strength.

Target 4 looks at three main strands in evaluation. One of these requires children to reflect on the way in which they have tackled the various aspects of the process — for example, their approach, planning, group work and interactions. A second looks at the outcomes of their work, the artefact, system or environment developed, and how well it performs its functions. The third concerns their exploration of the impact these outcomes may have on the original situation they were working in, and on the people affected. The first and third strands in particular create opportunities to develop equality issues. The process strand encourages evaluation of the behaviour and interactions of the children themselves. Evaluating impact involves the children in speculating about the potential effects of their ideas on as wide a range of different groups as possible, and developing attitudes and techniques to get real feedback from people wherever possible, rather than relying on (possibly) stereotyped views. Key questions may include, 'Who might be affected by your ideas?' 'How will they feel about this?' 'How could you find out what they think?'

Target 4 also includes the evaluation of the design and technological work of other people, through the same three strands. Since the world we experience is very largely the result of others' design and technology, intentional or not, this offers enormous scope. The children can evaluate almost anything: the fire alarm and evacuation system, local shops or traffic systems, yogurt pots. However, working on examples from other times and cultures, though most regularly suggested for equal opportunities work within design and technology, is actually hardest to do well. Children's evaluations are bound to come from their own perspective, and those of the small range of people they can identify with. Part of the function of design and technology is to give them the tools to extend their understanding further and further from themselves, but these skills and techniques build up slowly. It is often extremely difficult to find ways of involving children with the perspectives of the makers and users when working with unfamiliar cultural material. Stereotypes are more often reinforced than challenged.

Early Responses to Design and Technology in the National Curriculum

Awareness of the differences between the new design and technology, and the old CDT and science links is only slowly emerging. Many so-called design and technology resources are simply watered down repackaged imports from secondary CDT, previously sold as 'Primary CDT' and 'practical problem solving' materials. Usually, children are expected to use construction materials in some way to solve a predetermined problem, e.g. making a desk tidy, or a toy with moving parts. These activities offer the children useful experience, but do not meet all the objectives nor the spirit of the design and technology attainment targets: the children have no real part in exploring needs and opportunities or evaluating the human consequences of their solutions.

Currently, primary INSET and resources concentrate on 'making' skills to the exclusion of the other skills and knowledge required to teach the subject. There is a ready market for the predominantly male and subject-oriented trainers, who offer physical making skills to mainly female primary teachers. Meeting this perceived deficit in some teachers' skills may obscure other deficits elsewhere. Given the whole range of skills required to teach design and technology, it may well be that some male teachers require help in developing an explicit capability in traditionally female strengths — using processes to solve problems, organising groups, eliciting people's real opinions.

These issues also apply to the children. The over-simple assumption that girls 'need help with making' distracts attention from their already high capability in work related to Targets 1 and 4, and the relative lack of these skills in boys. These capabilities could be made more visible and more valued in the classroom, where the concentration on a perceived deficit in the girls may well obscure a very important deficit in the boys, and also perpetuate a view of technology that privileges the relatively high status of making. Defining teaching needs in this way contributes to the problem, not to the solution.

A Project on Clothes with 9–10 year-olds

The next section describes work that I was involved in as a primary advisory teacher in design and technology, working in a school whose whole-school project for the term was 'Clothes'. For brevity and clarity I have compressed the case study, and referred to 'the teacher'. In fact I am drawing from work I was part of in a number of classrooms, though everything I describe really happened. Working on the prescribed theme for the term — clothes — the teacher decided to start with clothes for school. She was concerned to find a starting point where both girls and boys would be able to contribute, and which was not eurocentric or 'machine-based'.

Her aim for the first phase was to ensure that all the children were involved and bringing their own ideas and experience to bear, so she devised two initial activities: a general discussion to get the children talking and contributing their ideas about clothes, followed by work in small groups to decide which aspects they would follow up. 'Clothes' is a project which draws on social issues. This is fortunate since it prioritises discussion of needs, values and wants, in which everyone can share. Rushing into making and constructing too early in a project can lead to boys dominating the activity, getting on with making, and losing touch with whether their ideas might actually be used by anybody.

During the discussion, the teacher deliberately drew in every child and asked for their point of view. She helped the children to disagree without dismissing each other's contributions, and looked for opportunities to talk about the range of views people held. She made her notes on a flip-chart, so that all the children could see what she was drawing and writing. The children mentioned arguments with parents, clothes getting torn and dirty, the cost, liking to wear nice things. A reference to wearing school uniform started a lively debate about wanting to be able to wear national clothes, and problems if some children had fewer nice clothes than others. They talked about the sorts of clothes that are sold for school, and looked at a couple of catalogues. The children tried to identify the difference between the 'school' clothes and the others.

Using the flip-chart as an aide-memoire, each small group now spent a few minutes negotiating what they wanted to find out more about, and how they would go about this. Moving from group to group, the teacher listened and joined in, encouraging them to listen to each other's contributions, asking them to justify statements, and explain how they would check their ideas and get further information. Many ideas were in fact generated from discussion at home or with other people, which gave the project wider perspectives than the teacher could have offered alone, and helped to incorporate the 'other times and cultures' requirement in AT4.

The next session began with brief presentations to the class from each group, explaining what they intended to do, and asking for comments and suggestions. The plans ranged from surveys of children within the school to find out their attitudes and wants, to questionnaires for parents about their views on school clothing and comparative costings of an outfit from the catalogues. As they carried out their tasks, the children began to think about various possibilities for further action. One group began to draw up criteria for a school uniform. Another started to put together a booklet of guidance for parents, explaining what the children would need for school. After initial comments from parents, this extended beyond clothing into ideas for swimming bags and suggestions for packed lunches. Two children thought that teachers should also have a uniform and made drawings, adding reasons why currently worn clothes were sometimes inappropriate. Meanwhile, a group had been discussing lost property, and devising a system they hoped would get it back to its owners, or at least ensure that it was sensibly used, as dressing up clothes 'for the little ones' or sent to a charity. One group who had found it difficult to develop an idea of their own were shown a sweatshirt sold by a neighbouring school. They then put forward their proposals for items for the school to sell, including pens and badges. They designed a school logo and listed costs and anticipated profits to present to the Head and Governors. The emphasis of many groups' work had shifted from the original 'clothes for school', but the teacher had seen this simply as a 'jumping off' point, not as a boundary on the children's work.

As the project started to run out of time, the teacher asked each group to develop a presentation of their ideas for the school and parents.

This cross-curricular project involved children in mathematics, humanities, personal and social education, language work, information technology and so on, and is an example of traditional good primary practice. What was distinctively 'design and technology' was the emphasis on the children themselves deciding on the problems or opportunities, formulating their own plans and designs, making their own decisions about what to do next and evaluating their own and other children's solutions.

The primacy given to the child's perspective, decision-making and judgement has important implications for equal opportunities. For much of the time, children in schools are in the position of learning what the teacher wants them to learn, in the way she decides to teach it. The outcome for many children is an education which is mostly based on other people's ideas of what is important. Many girls, children from minority groups, and children with disabilities or learning difficulties are 'invisible' in the ordinary curriculum, which generalises ideas, and so rarely shows them people and situations with which they can identify and empathise. Design and technology prioritises the children's own perspectives and the perspectives of their own community — the people they know and come into contact with. In addition, the teacher has the chance to step back, and learn about the children and their experience, from the children themselves.

Conclusion

The design and technology curriculum takes a broad view of technology, incorporating the ways problems are defined and the impact of solutions as well as designing and implementing them. This view has many implications for teachers as well as children. But in particular, good design and technology experience is empowering for children. It encourages them to recognise that they can have an effect on their environment. It can also help them develop attitudes that see that environment as the result of people's decisions in which they can take part, not as an unalterable, 'given' situation. This understanding can spread beyond the subject area and challenge practice in other subjects, school rules, relationships with teachers. Potentially, design and technology could change the way schools work!

10 Aprons and Attitudes: A Consideration of Feminism in Children's Books

SUE ADLER

This chapter on feminism in children's books challenges us to move beyond conventional views about sexism and anti-sexism, valuable and necessary though it still is to 'balance the books' and ensure that females and males are not portrayed in gender stereotypical roles. Sue Adler argues that children's literature has got stuck with 'anti-sexist' rhetoric. Adult feminist literature (which is never called anti-sexist) reflects 'womanist' values — rather than women trying to emulate men — and this perspective is needed for children's books.

Balancing the Books?

A true story. A five-year-old just home from a day at school accuses his mother of not being a real mother. Puzzled, she asks why not. 'Because', he says, 'you haven't even got an apron, and real mothers always wear aprons. It says so in our books'.

This anecdote, together with my readings of the many articles and books written on sexism in children's books in the 1970s and early 1980s, was a basis for much of my own work in the 1980s. In common with most feminists who worked on issues of gender in young children's books, I focused on sexism, looking at the gross under-representation and misrepresentation of girls and women. Most of the books showed (and still show) sex-stereotyped images of women and men, used (use) gender-biased language and were (are) androcentric, that is, they take male experience as the norm. Counting the numbers of female and male characters in text and illustrations; comparing the roles of females and males; discussing the attitudes and assumptions underpinning stories — all this work leads to an unrelenting picture of female oppression and marginalisation.

111

I am not arguing that such work was worthless or that it has no place today. I believe it is still relevant and necessary. But I think that it has limitations. It does not explore in any depth how sexism is really represented or perpetuated through books and suggests that equalisation of numbers of female/male characters and the establishment of androgynous work and domestic environments will lead to the elimination of sexism. I am sceptical that balancing the books will lead neatly to a redistribution of power or a re-imaging of power, although that does not mean we can or should opt out of the task of discussing issues in books with children and with providing them with the best possible models. Moreover, it is simplistic to assume that balancing or 'correcting' texts will easily change stereotyped thinking. Even if we all agreed that a 50/50 distribution by sex of the characters in children's books was something to strive for, would we agree what those characters should be shown doing, thinking or feeling? I doubt it. Also I do not believe that we should agree. Exchanging one monolithic view with another is not progress.

In an effort to provide girls with the same opportunities as those available to boys, there is a danger of strengthening the master's house by establishing his values and achievements as the most desirable ones. Valuing girls and women when they behave, or aspire to behave, like boys and men is no solution. Rather, it seems to me, this escalates the problem, with wide-ranging implications for education. The National Curriculum emphasises maths, science and technology; the education system favours training for the commercial and industrial workplace. Under the guise of widening options, are we pandering to a hierarchy in which the strengths and interests of many girls are sacrificed to the needs of a male-defined world? Where is the space for other views of the world?

Work on sexism in children's books usually takes a liberal and reformist line and rarely a radical approach. The assumptions of liberalism and equal opportunities which underlie much anti-sexist work tend to stress equality of access, but seldom acknowledge different starting points, interpretations, perceptions and values. This may not be as condescending as the well-meaning comment 'I treat them all the same' which overlooks diversity as well as individuality but it still ignores differently structured conceptual worlds. It also begs the question of norm — the same as whom? Children read as individuals, gendered, of course, and consequently I would say, there is a marked difference in the ways girls and boys read as well as in their reading preferences. Sex, class, ethnicity, culture, life-experience, age, ideas, even mood, all shape our understanding and interpretation of texts.

Working Towards a Definition of a Feminist Children's Book

The concept of feminism in children's books is problematic. Despite the wealth of material on adult literature and gender issues, sexuality, feminism and the construction of femininity, I have found little to parallel this with regard to children's literature. Indeed, I have heard (and myself had) doubts that feminism in relation to children's books was anything other than a consideration of sexism and anti-sexism. But recognising that problems do exist is neither new nor restricted to radical feminists. In reply to a question on what parents should do about sexism and racism in children's books, Margaret Meek replied, 'Read and think all the time. I am worried by the fact that some commentators fail to distinguish between the deep roots of these problems and their surface presentation. The mere fact of a heroine performing masculine feats is no guarantee that the author's values are sound ...' (Meek, 1982: 185)

Defining feminism

In a chapter entitled 'What is feminism?' in a book with the same title, Dale Spender writes:

'I think that feminism is based on a "better" set of assumptions than any other world view I have encountered. I think it is a fairer way of viewing and organising the world. I assume that human beings are equal; that we can learn to live in harmony with each other — and the planet — and that there is no necessity for violence, exploitation, persecution and war.' (Spender, 1986: 215)

Feminism, for this influential writer and educationalist, gives us a way to conceptualise the world in terms other than materialism and individualism. Feminism examines power relations, mainly (although not exclusively) between the sexes. In children's books, as in other areas of study, it is not an ideology of sexual difference that is at issue; it is assumptions about male superiority and female inferiority, the abuse of power, and androcentricity that should be under scrutiny. Feminism is not only concerned with the struggle for political and economic change but also with valuing women's experience, with notions (however idealistic) of sisterhood, and therefore with challenges to patriarchy. Beyond broad generalisations, there is no one view of feminism and significant differences as well as similarities between feminists flourish. (Discussion on varieties of feminism is outside the scope of this chapter and is well documented elsewhere, for example in Rosemary Tong's *Feminist Thought: A Comprehensive Introduction*, a book which highlights some of the main perspectives of feminist thought.)

Defining children's books

A non-sexist book

Rough definition

(1) A book about the dream of a society where sexism, categorisation and discrimination on the grounds of gender do not exist. (Marge Piercy explores this utopia in her adult science fiction novel *Woman on the Edge of Time*.)

(2) A book in which men and women, girls and boys, are shown in equal numbers, performing similar tasks and behaving similarly.

In a non-sexist book then, women and men, girls and boys would be shown doing equivalent things and would be equally represented. But it needs far more than equal numerical representation in children's books to address the problems of sexism and ultimately redress the balance.

An anti-sexist book

Rough definition: a book written to challenge sexist assumptions. The subtext 'gender' becomes the subject of the book. An anti-sexist book may deal with femininity, masculinity, or power relations between the sexes. Many anti-sexist books tackle stereotypical and limiting male gender roles, and the consequences of sexism for boys as well as girls. The author may be female or male.

Many anti-sexist books are, in my experience, best used with children older than the obvious age-group, to discuss gender issues.

A feminist book

Rough definition: A woman/girl-centred book, about women or girls, truthful about the reality of being female, showing both the upside and the downside. A feminist book is always anti-sexist and may overtly or covertly challenge sexism or misogyny. However, this is not necessarily the main theme or purpose of the book. It will give a female perspective. I think that feminist books (for any age) are written by feminists.

In proposing a feminist children's book we need to think through what it might mean to value and represent female experiences equally with male. Furthermore, it is undeniable that some women's work is disempowering at the moment and major structural changes in society would be required to re-evaluate it. Equally, many experiences can be depicted honestly through female eyes, but still say little to children about women's power to choose what they do and what happens to them.

These rough definitions raise the question of attribution and identity of authors and illustrators. Authors of books for adults are often given the opportunity to describe themselves and this is published on the book jacket. This is not usual with children's authors, so we do not always know whether the writer would claim to be feminist. Also, very few children's books in Britain are published by feminist presses — another clue some adult books give us to the author's political stance.

Books and articles about children's books

Looking to the literature for insights, the notable exceptions to the dearth of work on feminism and children's books are the analyses and publication of feminist fairy tales. Investigation into how meaning is constructed and given in fairy tales and how the stories influence children, is a serious area of study and research. Psychologists (e.g. Marie-Louise von Franz) and academics (e.g. Jennifer Waelti-Walters and Jack Zipes) have explored the role of fairy tales as models for feminine behaviour. Feminists have sought alternatives to oppressive fairy tales, compiling anthologies for children and adults. These make a real contribution to feminist literature, showing girls and women in roles other than beautiful victims or wicked witch/step-mothers, and relationships which are not competitive, manipulative or exploitative.

Bronwyn Davies' *Frogs and Snails and Feminist Tales* (1989) is the most recent and thorough book I have read on gender issues and young children's books. Davies provides an overview of feminist theory as well as details of her research with young children. The responses of girls and boys to *The Paper Bag Princess, The Princess and the Dragon, Oliver Button is a Sissy*, and *Rita the Rescuer* are documented and carefully analysed. The book is essential reading for those working with children and interested in the way gender is constructed.

In her discussion of stories themselves, Bronwyn Davies notes that feminist stories are generally of two kinds — those with the story about gender (or the subtext turned into the text) and those where the gender-relations remain as the subtext but a new narrative is created by altering the value system and gender roles. Sex-role reversal disrupts the narrative and may startle the reader into a serious consideration of who, based on sex, does what. She cites *Oliver Button is a Sissy* as an example of the first type; rewritten fairytales and the *Paper Bag Princess* as examples of the second kind (pp. 45–46).

Unlike Davies, I would described both these kinds of story as 'anti-sexist' and not as 'feminist'. Bronwyn Davies does not distinguish between anti-sexist (or non-sexist) and feminist literature. She lists as 'stories with an explicit feminist message' (p. 142) two books (out of four titles) about boys having to deal with societal stereotypes of appropriate male behaviour.

Many titles on her list are written and illustrated by men. I do not deny or wish to undermine the links between feminism and individual men's efforts to counter patriarchy (while still, willingly or not, benefiting from it) nor their attempts to reconstruct a less sexist space by recognising that they too are 'gendered'. The role of men — writers, publishers, teachers, librarians, parents, carers — as anti-sexist people, supportive of feminist ideals, is as relevant in discussion of children's books as elsewhere. But I do believe, as I mentioned above, that feminist books are written by women who consider themselves to be feminists.

My own interest in the subject of feminism in children's books, disappointment with some of the available analyses, and impatience with checklists and guides to assessing sexism in children's books has prompted me to continue thinking. I am influenced by Valerie Walkerdine who discusses how we — adults and children — draw meanings from the texts we read and images we see. She goes beyond the quantitative research on sex-bias, and draws on psychoanalytic theory to explore the ambiguous and often contradictory identities that are offered to girls. She moves the debate a long way from number crunching in an attempt to show how what girls choose to read (including comics, romances and general fiction) feeds and fulfils fantasies at the same time as defining the real limitations of the female role.

Working with Teachers on Distinguishing Anti-sexism and Feminism in Children's Books

I have been arguing in this chapter that there is an important distinction to be made between anti-sexism and feminism; not for the intellectual fun of it, but to find ways of working with children and enabling ourselves and them to clarify issues and move forward. In the past few years, I have tried to extend the agenda which typically sets out to analyse sexism and consider what constitutes anti-sexism, but seldom recognises or tries to promote feminism. In workshop sessions with teachers, I have used the following statement and question to provoke deliberation and debate:

> 'Anti-sexist' and 'feminist' are not synonymous terms. Nor are 'multi-cultural' and 'anti-racist' synonymous. For example, a book can be both multicultural and racist. What do these mean, in the context of book evaluation?
>
>> Sexist/Non-sexist/Anti-sexist/Misogynist/Feminist
>> Racist/Multi-cultural/Non-racist/Anti-racist/Homophobic
>> Written from a Black perspective
>> Written from a feminist perspective
>> Women's book

Participants discuss our loose use of the terms and how confused — and confusing — this is. Differences as well as similarities, overlaps and contradictions, can be explored in the exercise.

Some Examples of Anti-sexist and Feminist Children's Books

I have focused here on picture books showing families, and in particular on the portrayal of mothers, grandmothers and daughters, and independent women in my attempt to differentiate between anti-sexism and feminism. I have selected a very small number of titles as examples. The choice of titles is a bit arbitrary; there were many others I could have used but I hope that readers will find the issues raised transcend the individual titles. The aim is to open up the debate and raise issues — not to critique individual titles.

An example of an anti-sexist book

In *Piggybook* by Anthony Browne, to escape domesticity and servitude, Mrs Piggott leaves her husband and two sons for a short while. They came to realise how badly they have treated her, and how they took her labour for granted. The point about the value of women's work in the home is nicely made, as is that of male exploitation of women. The book directly — and deliberately — challenges that aspect of patriarchy relating to the position of women in the family.

The piglets/boys are just like their dad, copying his language to address their mother. They do not converse with her, they call out their demands. She does not say a word throughout the book. After she leaves, the language of father and sons gets more piglike. They communicate with each other by squealing, grunting and snorting their sentences. On her return, they snuffle, 'P L E A S E come back'.

The resolution of the problem is some task-sharing in the household.

'And they all helped with the cooking.'

'They actually enjoyed it!'

So, boys and men may help with the cooking while still perceiving this as the woman's task. Since it is a game to them they are likely to enjoy it. Significantly, the males in *Piggybook* are shown cooking together. This co-operative play could be contrasted with the lonely, tedious chore that cooking represents for many women.

We read that Mrs Piggott works outside the home, but it is clear, that unlike her husband, she does not have 'a very important job'. We are not told why she returns to her unloving family, but it is easy to assume that financial dependence is a factor. She remains trapped, although in the superb illustrations we see her exchange her dowdy skirt and jumper for bright dungarees; and her transformation from a (literally) featureless character to an individual.

The book has a happy ending. Mrs Piggott ends up smiling with a new solitary task — still alone, she mends her husband's car. There is no hint that she has taken this over from her husband: I speculate that she is doing it for fun and to escape from the house. Is this a simple case of 'males and females can each do the others work'? There is more than a hint of Mrs Piggott as Superwoman, capable of taking on anything. The role of women, exemplified here by Mrs Piggott, as paid workers, mothers, and unpaid domestic workers in their own homes is extended to motor mechanics.

Clearly, this is an anti-sexist book. Although its theme is a feminist issue, it is not a book I would describe as 'feminist'. As adult readers, we may recall feminist fiction dealing with women trapped in domesticity. Drawing on our understandings from adult feminist fiction can help to move the debate beyond countering blatant sexism to the questions — What might a feminist *Piggybook* look like? Could Mrs Piggott break out of her isolation? Get a different job? Seriously shift the power-base in the home?

Examples of feminist books

The Patchwork Quilt, by Valerie Flournoy, illustrated by Jerry Pinkeney, is one of my personal favourites. I like to read this book to children and often use it together with teachers when working on the use of picture books or fiction across curriculum areas. It is a warm family story, focused on a child, her grandmother and her mother. The illness of the grandmother and her incomplete quilt, a beautiful, useful and historically significant item, is part of the story line. Male characters are present in the book, shown sympathetically though not in central positions.

The first picture in the book shows mother and daughter in the kitchen. It is this that led some teachers in an outer London school to assert during an in-service training session that I was showing them a sexist and sex-role stereotyped book. I argued then — and now — that this is a feminist book, as strong in its feminism as many adult novels centred on women in the home. Mother, daughter and grandmother spend time sewing the quilt, and the story shows them cooking and baking for the Christmas celebration.

There is a thin line — and one I trend with some trepidation — between extolling feminine values and contexts, and slipping into traps made by biological determinists, eugenists and sexual fundamentalists. But feminist critics have redeemed 'homely detail'. Annette Kolodny (1986) notes that in the mid-nineteenth century, there was a vast market for (women's) literature ... 'which would treat the contents of their lives — the sewing circle rather than the whaling ship, the nursery rather than the lawyer's office — as functional symbols of the human condition' (p. 49).

In contrast, Sue Sharpe, author of the influential *Just Like A Girl: How Girls Learn to be Women* (published in 1976, reprinted frequently and still in print), describes the suburbia of children's books, pointing out (again) that males are portrayed as active and females as passive and domestic. But change, for Sharpe, has little to do with radical feminist perceptions. Equality with men and access to their activities, values and life-style are the issues for her. She writes 'There are very few successful women in our society and it is difficult to write drama and adventure stories about housewives and mothers' (p. 100). I argue that housewives and mothers have a dynamic part in children's books and that their representation is a key issue in considering feminism — or sexism, or anti-sexism — in the literature.

The apron as a symbol of the mother, in her narrow role as the housewife in servitude and drudgery, has been mentioned. The 'fault' lies with attitudes to women's work and worth, and the negative, low status connotations attached to domestic work, not with the garment itself or its wearer. The stereotypical image of a mother wearing her apron wherever she goes, with bland, mindless, smile remains powerful and frightening, relating not to what any mother really is, but to a projected idea of how some would like her to be. Clearly, not all books show mothers in such a negative light.

Sigrun Srivastava's *My Mother* is a book I came across more than ten years ago and which I still enjoy. This is how it starts:

I love my mother. I think my mother is the nicest mother in the world. She is tall, has long black hair and dark brown eyes. When she works with me in the garden, she wears blue jeans. But most of the time, she wears a saree.

Pupu and her mother are shown in the kitchen (where appropriately, she wears an apron), shopping, sewing, and knitting, gardening and painting the garden gate. Pupu's father is, we are told, an engineer. Pupu's mother, who can and does answer many questions, suggests he will tell his daughter about aeroplanes and machines. I do not interpret this as a sexist element in an otherwise anti-sexist book — I think it is a sensible comment on specialist knowledge. In any event, the child's wish to know could be interpreted as a counter to a sexist assumption about young girls' areas of interest.

The book counters sexism with its positive pictures of daughter and mother in a range of activities. Similarly, it counters racist stereotypes. But the spirit of the book is lost by a bald statement that it is 'positive and non-stereotyped'. The warmth and humour in the relationship between child and mother and the secure, loving home that is the basis of Pupu's life get lost in the jargon of equality, however worthy.

A *Chair for My Mother* by Vera B. Williams features a working class family — daughter, mother and grandmother — saving to buy a comfortable chair after a fire destroys their possessions. Narrated (again) by a young girl, it has the gentleness of the previous title. Co-operation, dignity and caring are key feminist elements in the book. Adult readers in search of 'anti-sexist' elements can point to the working mother and her boss, Josephine. Those looking for a truthful female perspective will find a wealth of material on women's experience — e.g. the illustration of a kitchen scene portraying the working mother after an exhausting day; the evidence in text and pictures of a close relationship between girl and grandmother. The clothes are worth examining — both mother and grandmother are rather elegant and always smart, the girl wears trousers except when shopping. There are two other books featuring the same family — each as commendable and with a similar 'feel' of valued female daily life.

A Chair for My Mother

Another example is not about family as such, but about an individual woman and sisterhood. *Louise Builds a House* by Louise Pfaffer tells, with minimal text and bright illustrations, the story of Louise's fantastic constructions. In my view it is a feminist book, not just an anti-sexist one with a 'women can build too' message. One reason for this is its focus on a woman and her imagination. Another is its final page, where Louise decides to give the house to her sister, showing sharing and sisterhood as aspects of feminism. Yet this is not a didactic book. It is vivid and light-hearted. Children love the details in the drawings — Louise's shoes are worth a second look. So while the book is useful for serious consideration on the serious subject of its text, building, and for its subtext, gender, it is also (and essentially) fun and funny.

Just Us Women by Jeannette Caines, illustrated by Pat Cummings, shows a girl and her aunt enjoying a day out together.

'Saturday morning is jump-off time. Aunt Martha and I are going to drive all the way to North Carolina in her new car. Aunt Martha says, "No boys and no men, Just us women".'

'I'd never use a book like that! It's sexist the other way!' — a real and angry response from a teacher. If one's theoretical framework is opposed to (a) valuing women/femininity and (b) respecting the need for women-only times and spaces, the title of this book is a hackle-raiser. The comment above, which I have heard echoed frequently, show that the mythology of 'sexism the other way' needs to be debunked. Excluding men is not the same as excluding women. All those books on library and bookshop shelves about Vikings, Romans, castles, etc are sexist by omission. Androcentricity is normalised to the extent that few people question it. Promoting a feminist view — all too rare an experience in children's books — is a long way from oppressing males.

Conclusions

It is time to reassess women's lives as shown in children's books, not because we have eliminated sexism but rather because it remains. As adult readers, we appear to have no problem accepting that adult feminist novels will have details on the home, clothes and food, and that many women's prime interest is in relationships. We are, it seems, quite relaxed about attaching the label 'feminist' (with its many meanings and nuances, and recognising its changing meanings) to adult novels published by the feminist presses and women who define themselves as feminists. We do not describe these adult books as anti-sexist. That label is reserved for children's books, where, quite nervously, we attempt to decode social messages and line them up neatly in a good/bad polarity: sexist versus anti-sexist;

racist versus anti-racist. Again, I am not suggesting that analysis of racism and sexism is not needed or valid — but I am suggesting it does not necessarily create a place for useful (and lively) debate on feminist perspectives and on Black perspectives.

So, what is your view of feminism in books for children? Isn't it time that feminism had a place in the discussions on children and their books? Isn't it time that children's books had a place in the discussions on feminism?

References and resources

References in text

Children's books

Browne, A. (1986) *Piggybook*. London: Magnet.

Caines, J.F. (1982) *Just us Women*. illus. by P. Cummings. New York: Harper and Row.

De Paolo, T. (1983) *Oliver Button is a Sissy*. London: Magnet.

Flournoy, V. (1985) *The Patchwork Quilt*. illus. by J. Pinkeney. London: Bodley Head.

Munsch, R.N. (1982) *The Paper Bag Princess*. illus. by Michael Martchenko. Leamington Spa: Scholastic.

Offen, H. (1985) *Rita the Rescuer*. London: Methuen.

Pfaffer, L. (1988) *Louise Builds a House*. London: Collins.

Strivastava, S. (1978) *My Mother*. New Delhi: Children's Book Trust.

Williams, V.B. (1983) *A Chair for My Mother*. London: Julia MacRae.

Wood, A. (1981) *The Princess and the Dragon*. London: Child's Play.

Adult books

Davies, B (1989) *Frogs and Snails and Feminist Tales: Preschool Children and Gender*. London: Allen and Unwin.

Kolodny, A. (1986) A map for re-reading: Gender and the interpretation of literary texts. In E. Showalter (ed.) *New Feminist Criticism: Essays on Women, Literacy and Theory*. London: Virago.

Meek, M. (1982) *Learning to Read*. London: Bodley Head.

Piercy, M. (1979) *Women on the Edge of Time*. London: The Women's Press.

Sharpe, S. (1976) *Just Like a Girl: How Girls Learn to be Women*. London: Penguin.

Spender, D. (1986) What is feminism? A personal view. In J. Mitchell and A. Oakley (eds) *What is Feminism?* Oxford: Blackwell.

Tong, R. (1989) *Feminist Thought: A Comprehensive Introduction*. London: Unwin Hyman.

Von Franz, M. (1972) *Problems of the Feminine in Fairytales*. New York: Spring.

Waelti-Walters, J. (1982) *Fairytales and the Feminine Imagination*. Quebec: Eden Press.

Walkerdine, V. (1984) Some day my prince will come: Young girls and the preparation for adolescent sexuality. In A. McRobbie and N. Mica (eds) *Gender and Generation.* London: Macmillan (also in Walkerdine, V. (1991) *Schoolgirl Fictions.* Verso.

Zipes, J. (1986) *Don't Bet On the Prince: Contemporary Feminist Fairy Tales in North America and England.* London: Gower.

Further reading

Children's Rights Workshop (1976) *Sexism in Children's Books: Facts, Figures and Guidelines.* Writers and Readers.

Davies, J. (ed.) (1981) *Sex Stereotyping in School and Children's Books.* London: Publishers Association.

Dixon, B. (1977) *Catching Them Young: Sex, Race and Class in Children's Fiction. London: Pluto.*

The English Centre, ILEA (1985) *The English Curriculum: Gender.* London: ILEA.

Joyner, J. (1986) Sexism in children's fiction. *Bookquest* 9, 1.

McFarlane, C. (1986) *Hidden Messages? Activities for Exploring Bias.* Birmingham: Development Education Centre.

Michel, A. (1986) *Down with Stereotypes: Eliminating Sexism from Children's Literature and School Textbooks.* Paris: Unesco.

National Association for the Teaching of English: Language and Gender Working Party (1985) *Alice in Genderland: Reflections on Language, Power and Control.* NATE.

Paul, L. (1987) Enigma variations: What feminist theory knows about children's literature. *Signal* 54, September, 186–202.

Peterson, S.B. and Lach, M.A. (1990) Gender stereotypes in children's books: Their prevalence and influence on cognitive and affective development. *Gender and Education* 2, 2.

Segel, E. (1986) As the twig is bent: Gender and childhood reading. In E.A. Flynn and P.P. Schweickart (eds) *Gender and Reading: Essays on Readers, Texts and Contexts.* Baltimore: John Hopkins.

Stinton, J. (ed.) (1979) *Racism and Sexism in Children's Books.* Writers and Readers.

Stones, R. (1983) *Pour out the Cocoa, Janet: Sexism in Children's Books.* London: Longman for Schools Council.

Zimet, S.G. (1976) *Print and Prejudice.* London: Hodder.

11 Assessment in Mathematics and Science: Issues for Teachers

ANNE QUALTER

This is the first of a set of three chapters looking at equal opportunities issues in assessment. Anne Qualter argues that there is pressure on primary teachers to use more formal methods of assessment, which may reproduce the systematic bias found in external assessment in other contexts. On the other hand, teachers' informal assessment is not unproblematical: the expectations we have of different pupils may affect judgments. While focusing on science and mathematics, Anne raises issues that will recur in the two later chapters on humanities and language: the need to pay attention to the nature of assessment tasks, the context in which children are assessed and children's own perceptions of the process; and the need to regard judgments as provisional and open to re-interpretation.

Introduction

It is generally accepted that we need to know how well children are doing and what they are learning so that we can make decisions about where they might go next. Assessment can be formative, to inform us about a child's progress so that we can plan future experiences for the child. Assessment can be summative, giving some sort of final score. The National Curriculum assessment system has, theoretically at least, run these two forms of assessment together. Teachers are asked to make assessments of their pupils for formative purposes and to use that information to construct summative assessments. By making the assessments teachers do for their own sake more 'High Stakes' (Gipps, 1990), that is, there is more riding on the assessments made, a new burden is being put on teachers to use more formal methods. These more formal methods may be of less use in classrooms, but they produce information that can be used for summative purposes (Harlen & Qualter, 1991).

If I am right in my argument that teachers are under pressure to use more formal assessments, it is worth considering what information we have, from other contexts, on the effects of this. How fair are external tests, for instance? What may bias the assessment? How can bias be counteracted? What might the advantages of teachers' own assessment be even for summative purposes? Although it does not necessarily follow that teacher assessment will reflect the bias of externally set assessment tasks, looking at what we know about such tests could help to highlight the pitfalls of assessment in terms of the possible threats to equal opportunities.

Exams and Tests

Traditionally examinations have been seen as a means of sorting children and comparing them with one another. Certain groups of children do better on public exams than others. Fewer girls than boys tend to achieve higher grades in maths and science exams. A lower proportion of pupils from ethnic minorities were entered for 'O' level exams (Eggleston *et al.*, 1986). Girls' performance in number tends to be equal to that of boys, but in other areas of mathematics such as practical problem-solving girls tend to fall behind (APU, 1985). Girls do as well as or better than boys on some aspects of science, but in other aspects boys do slightly better than girls at age eleven. These differences increase as pupils go through the secondary school. Girls tend to do better than boys on observation tasks, but in applying physics concepts and using certain measurement instruments boys have an increasing advantage (Johnson & Murphy, 1986). There is evidence to show that West Indian pupils do not do as well as their Asian, English, Scottish and Welsh counterparts: this has been found to be the case even when factors such as socio-economic status and ability, as measured by standardised tests, have been taken into account (Smith & Whetton, 1988).

All the results described above come from externally set tests, but what we need to know in order to learn from this is whether the tests can be taken as a true representation of a pupil's ability, or not. Do pupils sitting these tests have an equal opportunity to show what they know, understand and can do? In science there is a great deal of evidence to show that test items can be biased in favour of boys or girls; there is less research on the subject in terms of pupils from ethnic minorities. How a question is asked is an important factor in determining how successful a pupil will be. Multiple choice questions, for example, favour boys while open-ended tasks tend to favour girls.

How Assessment Tasks Influence Outcomes

If pupils are asked a science question which is set in a social or caring context girls are likely to do better than boys. If a science question is set in the context of cars and engines then 13-year-old boys are more likely than 13-year-old girls to do well, even if the science in each question is the same (Murphy, 1989). Pupils are therefore influenced by the way a question is asked. Although it is less widely recognised, the context and mode of presentation of maths questions does have an influence on how pupils interpret the task and therefore on the strategies they use to solve the problem set (Denvir, 1989). However, in maths and science the problem is more complex than simply the content or the context in which the tasks are set: it is also important how pupils feel about the subject, and whether they see it as appropriate to themselves. Science, for example is generally presented as the preserve of white, middle-class men. For girls, and pupils from cultures other than European, science can be seen as inappropriate, or just irrelevant.

The link between assessment in the formal context of exams and tests and the less formal context of the classroom should be clear. How we present the tasks we are assessing children on could have an important influence on how individual children respond. The same is of course true of teaching. How we present learning activities must influence how pupils engage with the activities. A pupil is more likely to do better at a task if she is interested in it. The same is true, it seems, for tasks set as assessments. In exams, or tests of any sort, all the pupils to be assessed are given the same questions. This could be seen as being fair to the test, and not necessarily fair to the individual pupil. If each pupil could be given a task which would interest her, was relevant to her and in which her way of answering the question was considered valid, then we would be being fair to the pupil rather than to the test. This is a possibility in teacher assessment which is not available to external assessors. However, the desire to make teacher assessment more like external assessment, so that it can be used for summative purposes could undermine this particular advantage of teacher assessment.

When Do Differences Begin?

Although measurable differences in science and maths between girls and boys do not tend to emerge much before the age of eleven, other differences in the ways pupils engage with the subjects are apparent from the time children begin school. Pupils are taught to behave in particular ways so that by the time they get to nursery school they tend to play in different ways. Girls are encouraged to develop their caring and homemaker skills by being given dolls and household toys; boys are given cars and building toys. Later on boys are much more likely than girls to be bought a computer, even when girls express a desire to have one (Gribbin, 1986). Girls' lack of experience with construction toys for example, and their lack of confidence with them is thought to adversely affect their ability to solve practical mathematical and scientific problems later on. Differences emerge, for example, between girls and boys in their ability to use certain measuring instruments as they grow older. It was on those instruments on which boys said they had more experience, such as ammeters and stop clocks, that they did well (Murphy, 1989).

If a teacher insists that girls take their turn with the construction toys she also needs to provide the pupils with a purpose by suggesting something they might like to build. This is because girls need to see the relevance of a task to themselves. At first the girls don't do as well as the boys, but they soon catch up when given the right stimulus.

Harding & Sutoris (1987) has suggested that because children are taught to attend to different aspects of their world they learn to learn in different ways, that is they develop different cognitive styles. This goes some way to explaining why, when given the same problem to solve, children interpret it in different ways. A number of children from the age of seven upwards were asked to design a boat to go around the world. Girls drew a boat shape and focused on what the cruise liner should have in it, bedrooms, kitchen, leisure facilities, but rarely an engine. Boys' boats were mostly devoid of the necessities of life, but did have a power source, and almost invariably had a weapon installed (Murphy, 1989). Having designed their boat the children were then given lolly sticks, silver paper, bits of fabric, straws and modelling clay with which to make a model of it. This was a relatively easy task for the boys who had concentrated on the shape of the boat. However, many girls were at a loss as to how to use the materials to model kitchens, multi-gyms, and such like. When asked to test their boats the boys could do so, whilst the girls could not. Often in science and technology, we only ask pupils to do the last part of this. In assessing pupils we may only ask them to tell us how they would design a fair test. Thus we are disadvantaging those children who do not interpret the problem in the way we expected them to.

Teacher assessment, free of the need to use fixed tests, should be a much fairer way of finding out what children know, understand and can do. However, it is important to recognise that the teacher's expectations can operate to the disadvantage of some pupils and the advantage of others. Girls are expected to be passive, good at language, but not so good at science and mathematics (these being hard, masculine subjects). West Indian children are often considered livelier than others, and may not be expected to be very good at mathematics. Any pupil with a poor command of English may not be expected to do well in science, particularly because of the need to record results. Research shows that, even when ability on entry is controlled for, pupils from ethnic minorities tend to be placed in a lower ability band by their teacher than is appropriate (Wright, 1987; Mortimore *et al.*, 1988). Although we tend to teach pupils in mixed ability classes in primary schools, we often group them according to our own assessment of the pupils' ability. Gipps (1990) suggests that, with the introduction of the National Curriculum there could be a move towards grouping children by their assessed level. Such grouping can only be equable if the process used to assess pupils and the decisions made about what to do about that assessment are equitable.

But What About Teacher Assessment?

It cannot be denied that external assessment is bound to be biased in some way or other. However, simply for practical purposes most of the data provided for each individual child for summative assessment at seven and eleven will come from the teacher. In the early days of the development of the age seven SATs the STAIR consortium gathered the most detailed teacher assessment data. They concluded that there was a tendency on the part of teachers to assess girls as higher than boys on English, but not for maths and science. In comparison to the SAT it seemed that teachers had overestimated girls' performance in English, whilst having a slight tendency to award fewer girls a level three in maths and science than the SATs did (STAIR, 1991). The NFER identified a trend for teachers to assess pupils from ethnic minorities lower than other children. The CATS consortium reported that ethnic minority children tended to do better on the SAT than teacher assessment. Making comparisons between teacher assessment and SAT results is problematic. Which is the most accurate? The discussion so far has suggested external assessments are likely to be biased, so there are problems in using the SATs as a yardstick against which to measure the quality of teachers' assessment. However, it does ring warning bells when the SAT data suggests smaller differences between girls and boys and between pupils from ethnic minorities and their schoolmates than teachers' own assessment indicates.

It could be that teachers' assessments in the early days of National Curriculum were based less on their actual assessments than they might now be. Eggleston (1988) felt that the introduction of teacher assessment against set criteria would be just what was needed to redress the balance of bias against black children and provide a firm basis for planning work with pupils.

Conclusion

The introduction of teacher assessment could mean that the bias which is almost inevitable in externally set tests is removed. However this will only be the case if teachers use assessment in a formative way, as part of teaching. It is perhaps appropriate here to look at one classroom assessment situation. A group of four five-year-olds were busily using flat coloured shapes to make a rocket shape on the floor; I joined in (Qualter, 1990). As each child picked up a piece I asked her to tell me either the shape or the colour. After a while the children automatically said what shape and/or colour each piece was. One child obviously had problems with the colours, and the shapes. Why was this? Was it colour blindness (he was a boy)? Or language problems (his first language was not English)? Or that he did not know his colours, and shapes? As we went on the children were learning their colours and shapes or consolidating their knowledge. The boy mentioned above was, by the time the rocket was complete, able to tell me the colours of the pieces, but needed more practice with the shapes. It seemed that he had known his colours and was learning their English names, whilst he probably did not know the shapes, but was beginning to learn them. This assessment was opportunistic, it fitted into something the children were enjoying doing. Had this been a more formal assessment, where children were all asked to name some colours and name some shapes then I would not have been able to disentangle the reasons why the child had problems. He would have been recorded as not meeting the relevant criteria at level 1 in maths and science.

The move towards more formal assessment by teachers in order to comply with the requirement to provide summative data could well lead to built in bias. Certainly teachers in special schools are very worried that their means of assessing their pupils will not be valued once the SATs really begin:

> 'My pupils won't be able to cope with the tests, so all the work we have done in science, and all the things they have learned will count for nothing.' (teacher in special school)

On the other hand a teacher needs to know more than whether her pupils meet the many and limited criteria of the National Curriculum. Because children can react differently to the same tasks we need to know about the whole child in order to plan work which will suit them all. However this brings its own dangers: there is the possibility that the effect of stereotypes and low expectations of particular groups might be made 'official'. That is, the data looks scientific because there is a number on it, but how we make decisions about what learning experiences to give a child is not made explicit.

There is no simple answer to the problem of ensuring equality of opportunity, however it is clear that making teacher assessment more like external tests is not the answer. Assessment for teaching requires sensitivity to the individual, an understanding of children's needs and open-mindedness. If assessment in the National Curriculum is to be successful and truly formative then we need to be aware of the pitfalls. In maths and science there are several ways in which we can introduce bias. Good quality INSET should be part of the agenda for ensuring that all teachers are aware of the problem and don't fall into the traps. The opportunities are there to enhance equal opportunities, but it would be foolish to assume that by merely legislating for teacher assessment you can make this happen.

References

Assessment of Performance Unit (1985) *A Review of Monitoring in Mathematics: 1978 to 1982.* London: HMSO.

CATS (1991) *The Pilot Study of Standard Assessment Tasks for Key Stage 1: A Report by The Consortium for Assessment and Testing in Schools (CATS).* London: SEAC.

Denvir, B. (1989) Assessment purposes and learning in mathematics education. In P. Murphy and B Moon (eds) *Developments in Learning and Assessment* (pp. 277–89). London: Hodder and Stoughton.

Eggleston, J., Dunn, D., Anjabli, M. and Wright, C. (1986) *Education for Some.* Stoke on Trent: Trentham Books.

Eggleston, J. (1988) The new education bill and assessment: Some implications for Black children. *Multicultural Teaching* 6(2), 24–30.

Gipps, C. (1990) *Assessment: A Teachers Guide to the Issues.* London: Hodder and Stoughton.

Gribbin, M. (1986) Boys muscle in on the keyboard. In L. Burton (ed.) *Girls into Maths Can Go* (pp. 117–21). London: Holt Education.

Harding, J. and Sutoris, M. (1987) An object relations account of the differential involvement of boys and girls in science and technology. In A. Kelly (ed.) *Science for Girls?* Milton Keynes: Open University Press.

Harlen, W. and Qualter, A. (1991) Issues in SAT development and the practice of teacher assessment. *Cambridge Journal of Education* 21 (2), 141–51.

Johnson, S. and Murphy, P. (1986) *Girls and Physics: Reflections on APU Survey Findings.* London: APU.

Mortimore, P., Simmons, P., Stoll, L., Lewis, D. and Ecob, R. (1988) *School Matters: The Junior Years.* Hove: Lawrence Earlbaum Associates.

Murphy, P. (1989) Gender and assessment in science. In P. Murphy and B. Moon (eds) *Developments in Learning and Assessment* (pp. 323–26). London: Hodder and Stoughton.

NFER/BGC (1991) *The Pilot Study of Standard Assessment Tasks for Key Stage 1: A Report by NFER/BGC Consortium.* London: SEAC.

Qualter, A. (1990) Assessing five years olds — Where do we start?' *Education 3-13* 18(3), October, 20–6.

Smith, P. and Whetton, C. (1988) Bias reduction in test development. *The Psychologist* July.

STAIR (1991) *The Pilot Study of Standard Assessment Tasks for Key Stage 1: A Report by the STAIR Consortium.* London: SEAC.

Wright, C. (1987) Black students — White teachers. In B. Troyna (ed.) *Inequality in Education.* London: Tavistock.

12 Assessing Humanities: Some Notes

PAT HUGHES

The humanities have often been a controversial area of the curriculum. Pat Hughes argues that the teaching of humanities is bound up with values — which immediately raises the question of whose values should form the basis of teaching, learning and assessment. Pat discusses the status of humanities as a subject, and how the way it is taught and assessed can contribute to inequalities based on gender, 'race' and class. She argues that an equal opportunities perspective should 'permeate both curriculum content and assessment', and provides an example of how pupils may make their own assessments of their work.

Relatively little is known about how children learn 'subjects' such as history and geography. Much more is known about how they learn maths, science and English. Certainly there has been considerable evidence of the lack of time spent on humanities teaching (Alexander, 1992) and the priority given to it by teachers (Ashton *et al.*, 1975). This lack of knowledge about learning humanities subject matter is reflected in its assessment, which has at primary level rarely merited more than a passing mention.

The Education Reform Act changed this. Initially it was intended that all the core and foundation subjects should be tested at 7, 11, 14 and 16. As it became obvious that this was virtually impossible the foundation subjects such as geography and history were dropped from the statutory assessment. At meetings held by NCC officers it became clear that non-mandatory tasks would be developed and teachers would be advised to use these.

At the time of writing one can only speculate about the nature of the tasks and perhaps more importantly whether already harassed teachers will want to increase their workload.

An Equal Opportunities Perspective to Learning Humanities

It is within this framework of doubt about assessing humanities that this chapter is written. While the systematic recording of children's activities is to be welcomed, assessing their progress in humanities raises very real questions in my mind. Affective and cognitive dimensions are involved; in the past people were urged to study humanities to learn values (Campbell & Little, 1989). The question immediately arises of whose values are to be learned and assessment should therefore look at the values themselves as well as the practicality of assessing values. The traditional Eurocentric nature of the humanities curriculum (Carrington & Troyna, 1988; Hughes, 1991; Wiegand, 1992) needs challenging. Equal opportunities perspectives are intrinsic to the knowledge deemed worthy of inclusion in the humanities curriculum. Much of the initial controversy about the content of the national curriculum documents for geography and history related to their relatively narrow and conventional view of the subject.

When this is related directly to assessment it is possible to see that if the values to be learned are alien to some pupils, they may suffer under assessment procedures. If their traditional stories, myths, legends and understandings of the past are not represented in the school curriculum their historical knowledge will be assessed as wanting. If their holiday destinations are to areas left out of the geography curriculum (Wiegand, 1992) their geographical knowledge of places will be assessed as deficient.

An equal opportunities perspective to humanities teaching should involve providing children with learning experiences, evidence, materials etc. which can be reconstructed or interpreted in the light of their 'own experience, judgments and discussion' (Campbell & Little, 1989). When teachers share children's experience teacher assessment is very much easier than when the experience is not shared and may not even be recognised. A good example is the strong criticism given by many teachers when pupils are reported to 'disappear' to Pakistan for a couple of months. The educational value of such travel is assessed negatively in terms of what will have been forgotten, rather than what will be learned. Assessment in terms of experience is very much harder than it at first seems. Realistically it may be impossible. It is very much easier to find out how well children can reproduce what has been identified as important for them to learn.

The Low Status of Humanities

The low priority formerly given to humanities teaching in the primary school is indicated most clearly in the general lack of information and support for recording and assessment. For this reason the non-mandatory tests, which are still being piloted at the time of writing, are particularly important in terms of content and knowledge about how children learn humanities.

HMI have been critical about humanities teaching in primary school (DES, 1985) but have limited their comments about gender issues to more general matters of classroom management (Hughes, 1991). *Curriculum Matters 11: History from 5 to 16* (DES, 1988) recognised that planning should 'pay greater attention than was formerly the case to the position of minority groups and the role of women in history', but takes this no further in terms of assessment. There is little data collection to show the relationship between written content and comprehension so it is difficult to know what influence this will have on pupil performance. Existing evidence in relation to gender tends to show that the invisibility of women in reading texts does not prevent girls from performing better than boys.

Robin Alexander's evaluation of the Primary Needs Programme in Leeds (Alexander, 1992) notes that girls were less likely than boys to be on task when doing 'topic' work and this was in contrast to every other area of the curriculum. It was also noted that, in environmental studies, pupils who were rated above average by teachers worked much less hard and were much more frequently distracted than those rated average or below. Alexander does not draw out the gender implications of this, which could be that girls performing well in other subjects perform less well in humanities. They certainly appear from his evidence to be showing less interest than boys. No comments are made on class or race implications, although earlier Alexander notes that there was considerable confusion among primary teachers and heads about multicultural and multi-ethnic education and a general tendency to equate one with the other.

The Leeds survey also showed that primary humanities work tended to be less demanding than work in other areas of the curriculum, and that this freed the teacher to concentrate on other curriculum areas.

There is no reason to believe that primary schools in Leeds are significantly different from schools in other parts of the country. The traditional low status of humanities teaching linked with the overload on primary teachers is more than likely to result in most schools deciding that the pressures on assessment are already heavy enough, and humanities assessment will not be given the priority that assessment in the core subjects has been given. It is ironic that those interested in humanities teaching should be placed in the invidious position of arguing for increased assessment in order to ensure that their area is well taught.

Assessing Geography and History

The low status of geography and history has resulted in a complex struggle by historians and geographers to enhance the importance of their particular field. This in turn has important consequences for assessment. Geography has moved from being an arts subject to a science. This change in emphasis has been successful in enhancing the status of geography but has meant that far more girls have dropped the subject at secondary school. Geography as a science means that gender-related issues in connection with geographical assessment are likely to be similar to those found in science and mathematics:

- the boy/girl-friendly content of questions and tasks set;
- ability to resource adequately so that girls are able to use instruments and materials and do not have endlessly to 'wait their turn';
- out of school experience which reinforces geographical knowledge, concepts, skills and understandings (Hughes, 1988).

All three points relate to skills learning and class and 'race' perspectives are also bound up in these arguments. The racist environment in which many black pupils operate means that their environmental awareness is likely to be limited to 'safe' areas. The opportunity to travel both abroad and in the UK is heavily dependent on finance and this will influence the types of out of school experiences available to many children. Some children may be entirely dependent on school educational visits to extend their geographical and historical understandings.

Even work within the school catchment area may have to be limited. In some schools it is actually dangerous to take children on a local environmental awareness trail. Few schools are willing to take up the environmental concerns of children about dog muck and condoms, although a recent Blue Peter programme featured a school which had done exactly that and looked at strategies to educate the general public through a Child to Child Project (Knowsley Primary School, 1991).

Historians have moved their subject from the Gradgrind approach to knowledge to the belief that children need to learn to become historians themselves. This means that children need to understand the skills and concepts involved in being a historian. Assessment is no longer related only to knowledge recall, but also to the understanding of knowledge — for example the reliability of historical sources. Again, it needs to be questioned how easy this is to assess with very young children.

There are likely to be gender-related issues in the assessment of history that are similar to those found in English:

- talk and discussion tends to be dominated by boys and so assessments may be made which relate more to a child's gender position in a group than to her/his ability.
- boys have more problems listening to others and may therefore have difficulty with key historical skills such as empathetic understanding.

Teacher Judgments

As the Orders stand at the moment there are obvious equal opportunities implications in assessment arrangements in the humanities, which state that for Key Stages 1 and 2 'assessment should be based entirely on teachers' own judgments of pupils' classroom work'. Research over many years has shown that teachers can be biased against particular children on grounds of social class, social attitudes, ethnic grouping, gender and special needs (Blyth, 1990). Blyth reviews research into the actual social processes that influence teachers' thinking about individual children, and teachers' consequent actions. When attitudes towards different children become 'entrenched' in teachers' everyday procedures they are bound to affect how children are assessed (Blyth, 1990).

Teachers' judgments about their pupils' progress are also informed by their own experience of assessment. For the majority of primary teachers their memories of assessment in both history and geography are tests and exams which were concerned with how much subject knowledge could be recalled. In the past, school-based knowledge of particular historical and geographical facts and figures was seen as uncontentious: the view was that every pupil could and should be equipped with a given cultural package. Interestingly enough this dates back to the time when both subjects had higher status than they do today because the cultural package was concerned with the growth, development and servicing of the British Empire. As teachers ourselves we need support in examining the equal opportunities dimensions of humanities teaching in order to help pupils' interpretation of historical sources.

The breakup of the USSR has shown how clearly the political climate influences our interpretation of events. The current political climate in this country is likely to contribute to a particular package of facts being seen as uncontentious. Teacher assessment may be influenced by these experiences so that the skills, concepts and understandings of historical and geographical context are not assessed.

Outside Factors Involved in Assessment

More generally assessments may be influenced by other factors largely outside teachers' control. Major publishers (Ginn, Longman, Heinemann, Simon & Schuster, Oxford University Press, and Oliver & Boyd) are responding to the demand for historical and geographical material for Key Stage 1 and Key Stage 2 with the provision of non-fiction reading books. Wiegand (1992) provides a fascinating insight into the politics behind publications for children and although the discussion is not directly related to equal opportunities issues it has important implications for resourcing.

If history and geography become subsumed as part of a language programme, boys who have greater difficulties with reading may have real problems relating to a resource which looks remarkably like a reading scheme. Historical and geographical materials produced under these auspices may be seen as fiction rather than fact and treated as such by pupils, who might otherwise be interested in something which looked more like a traditional reference book, where the skills for information collection are significantly different.

The commercial conservatism of most publishing houses ensures that publication is traditional. Many of these publications build in assessment procedures. These, like the contents of the material, need to be used with caution. Complex tick sheets are unlikely to have been designed by practising primary teachers, and their overall usefulness questioned. Ginn, for example, suggests this method of assessment, but makes no mention of any problems involved in it.

Planning grids adapted for pupil use are one way in which pupils themselves can record what they have actually done and teachers can assess this in terms of National Curriculum requirements. This provides an openness about assessment which is frequently absent in the literature. Pupils are surprisingly honest about how they have worked, what they feel they have learned and its general relevance to their lives. If we are serious about equal opportunities issues we need to acknowledge pupils' own evaluations and use these, together with our own, to make an overall assessment of performance. Children who underachieve — and as Alexander shows these are frequently those of high ability as well as low ability — are then challenged as to the reasons for this.

The sample grid below enables pupils to see the overall plan — in this case a History Study Unit — and identify their own learning within it.

Assessment relating to important cross-curricular skills involved in humanities (e.g. looking at photographs) could be recorded over the long term using a grid system to encourage both geographical and historical

PUPIL RECORD SHEET

NAME OF PUPIL:.. YEAR:.............. CLASS:...........
TITLE OF HISTORY UNIT:... TERM:............

Key Issues	Historical Concepts covered	Content	Resources, types of sources	Activities	Recording & Assessment A.Ts

skills acquisition. Assessing primary humanities is at an early stage. Those interested in equal opportunities issues need to ensure that they permeate both curriculum content and assessment.

References

Alexander, R. (1992) *Policy and Practice in Primary Education.* London: Falmer.
Ashton, P., Kneen, P. and Davies, F. (1975) *Aims into Practice in the Primary School.* London: Macmillan.
Blyth, A. (1990) *Making the Grade for Primary Humanities.* Milton Keynes: Open University Press.
Campbell, J. and Little, V. (1989) *Humanities in the Primary School.* London: Falmer.
Carrington, B. and Troyna, B. (1988) *Children and Controversial Issues.* London: Falmer.
DES (1985) *History in the Primary and Secondary Years: An HMI View.* London: HMSO.
DES (1988) *Curriculum Matters II: History from 5 to 16.* London: HMSO.
Hughes, P. (1988) Time to get girl friendly. *Times Educational Supplement* 4.12.87.
Hughes, P. (1991) *Gender Issues in the Primary Classroom.* London: Scholastic.
Weigand, P. (1992) *Places in the Primary School.* London: Falmer.

13 Assessing Language

JOAN SWANN

This chapter begins with an account of the diversity of language experience children bring with them into the classroom. But it argues that children's language experiences are not simply different: some varieties of language are more highly valued than others; the degree of continuity between home and school language use also varies between different children. The chapter illustrates how such factors may affect assessment — both in English and other curriculum areas.

Introduction

Children come to school with a diversity of language experiences, and a range of knowledge about language. Such experiences and knowledge will affect the ways children use language in the classroom, their perceptions of classroom activities and their readiness to participate in different activities. The ways children speak (the accent or dialect they use, their home or community language) will also affect how they are responded to by others — both teachers and other children. Differences between children may lead to inequalities in assessment: for instance, there may be a mismatch between certain children's language experiences and the experiences on offer at school; there is also a danger that judgements of children's competence (in 'English' and in other areas of the curriculum) may be affected by the language or language variety they speak.

In this chapter I shall first consider the implications of diversity in language for teacher assessment — in terms of children's different language experiences; particular issues relating to bilingual children; and how different languages, or language varieties are perceived. I shall then look at the need to devise assessment contexts and formats that take account of diversity.

Diversity in Language

Children's language experiences

In *Read it to me Now!* Hilary Minns (1991) documents the out-of-school experiences of five young children: Gurdeep, Gemma, Anthony, Geeta and Reid. Each child has different experiences of literacy in the home which, Hilary Minns argues, are embedded in their family's social and cultural traditions. They encounter, variously, 'print that is to do with shopping, recipes, sending off for things; looking up information in books, or checking stolen car numbers, reading and studying a sacred text; watching parents doing accounts and writing letters; the ritual of the bed-time story' (p. 107). Because of their different experiences, children have different perceptions of reading and what this entails. Sometimes there is a mismatch between what children have learnt at home and what they are expected to do at school.

The texts available in school, and the ways these are used, are not culturally neutral. Gurdeep, Gemma, Anthony, Geeta and Reid come into a classroom containing well-known children's stories such as *The Elephant and the Bad Baby, Rosie's Walk, The Jolly Postman, Each Peach Pear Plum, The Snowman.* Minns comments:

> 'Authors are writing books like these within a specific cultural frame- work and with a particular audience in mind — notably the hypothetical child reader who is socialised into responding to a story by making a conversation out of it. Their books are presented in ways which encourage the child to ask questions about the story, to predict what will happen next and to match what does happen against experiences in their own lives; the books require them to investigate and use their imagination, to stop and discuss and to interpret the words of the author. This presupposes a way of reading which is not shared by everyone and tensions can be set up between child, teacher and parent if there is a cultural mismatch about the way in which a book is to be read and understood by a child.' (p. 112)

Minns suggests that teachers need to be aware of the experiences children bring with them into school in order to monitor their progress and develop and extend their reading — to help them 'become literate in the fullest sense'.

Such comments don't just apply to reading. Children's prior experiences (out of school, in previous classes) will affect their perceptions of writing, and the ways they contribute to class and group discussion. They will also affect what children choose to read, write and talk about — and how confident they feel about dealing with different tasks and topics. As well as individual differences between children, there may be systematic differences between groups of children: for instance, between girls and boys; children from different class backgrounds and children from different ethnic groups.

It's necessary to recognise children's different language experiences in order to plan appropriate learning activities and to broaden the range of their reading and writing, speaking and listening. But children's different experiences also point to the danger of bias in setting assessment tasks and in the criteria used to assess children. It is likely that children will perform better on tasks of which they have had experience. Children will also have expectations about a task (for instance, whether it's appropriate for a girl or boy) and they will find different tasks more or less interesting. These factors too are likely to affect their performance.

Bilingual children

If we truly value children's linguistic competencies we will take the trouble to find out what they do know about language. If we don't value their linguistic competencies, neither they nor their parents are likely to tell us what they know. (Helen Savva, 1991, 'Bilingual by rights')

In order to find out what children know about language it's necessary to take account of the range of languages, or language varieties at their disposal. In the case of bilingual children this will involve the use of two, or perhaps more, languages to fulfil a variety of communicative functions. Bilingual children are unlikely to have identical competence in each language — one language will be stronger in certain areas, another in different areas. Children may well switch between languages during a conversation. The evidence we have of bilingual children's learning suggests that they should be encouraged to make use of all the languages at their disposal. If the emphasis is on learning and using English *at the expense* of other languages, particularly children's first language, there is a danger of underestimating bilingual children's achievements — both their knowledge of different curriculum areas, and their linguistic competence. Helen Savva tells the story of a boy, recently arrived from Bangladesh, who was withdrawn from his maths lesson for 'extra maths'.

'After completing a series of elementary calculations which the teacher provided, he pushed himself angrily from the table, chalked a complex algebraic equation on the blackboard and said "In Bangladesh, me!"' (1991: 9)

Bilingual assessment cannot simply be tacked on to a monolingual curriculum. In order to gain a picture both of bilingual children's language use and their competence in different curriculum areas it is necessary to find ways of supporting bilingualism in the classroom. Sharan-Jeet Shan gives the following suggestions for teachers who don't share pupils' languages to provide a positive language environment at Key stage 1:

- positively encouraging all pupils to use their first language, teaching and translating for each other in classroom and school;
- structuring working groups where possible to provide peer support in language, both in English and translating mother tongue;
- embedding concepts in structured and practical tasks so that completion is a visible demonstration of understanding;
- clear instructions and demonstration by the teacher, combining learning materials with verbal and nonverbal communication;
- close observation of pupils to see if they are engaged with the task: are they enjoying it, what is their general body language, their eye-contact with peers? Is attention sustained, are they joining in, handling the materials, helping to carry out the task, taking a lead, making attempts at discussion in their first language or in English ...? (1990: 17)

It is regrettable that the national curriculum, with its emphasis on teaching, learning and assessment in and through English, seems to regard bilingualism (in certain languages) as a short-term problem rather than a continuing educational benefit.

Perceptions of language

It's well known that we tend to make judgements about people based upon the way they speak. Someone speaking with a regional accent of English may be rated as less intelligent than someone whose accent is closer to 'received pronunciation' (the prestigious accent associated with middle-class speakers); minority languages spoken in the UK often have lower status than English, and this will affect the way their speakers are perceived. There are also differences in the ways girls and boys use language. Teachers' perceptions of girls and boys will be bound up with their speaking styles (girls may appear more polite, or uncertain of themselves and boys more forceful and self-confident), and there may be penalties for going against these expectations: what is 'confident' in a boy may be 'pushy' in a girl, for instance.

Such routine perceptions pose particular problems for the assessment of spoken language — a fact that has been recognised by the Cox Committee:

'Children should be judged on what they can do and on what they know, not on who they are [...]'

But

> 'The possibility of bias arises especially in the assessment of oracy, because of the difficulty of separating pupils' spoken language from perceptions of their personality and background.' (DES/WO, 1989: paras 11.9 and 11.11)

Perhaps not surprisingly, Cox gives no specific suggestions for the avoidance of this problem — such subtle biases are hard to tackle precisely because they operate below the level of conscious awareness. Simply making oneself aware of the danger of bias is one way of lessening its impact. There is a need constantly to interrogate judgements about children, and also to regard them as provisional. Patricia Murphy writes:

> 'Even with the knowledge a teacher builds up of an individual, views about what a child's actions or responses might mean about what the child thinks and knows should always be tentative.' (1991: 34)

Nowhere is this more true than in the assessment of spoken language.

Making Assessments

Assessment contexts

The notion of 'communicative effectiveness' underpins the assessment of English in the national curriculum: there is a concern with children's ability to use spoken language appropriately in different situations, to produce different kinds of writing and to read an increasing range of texts. The specifications of what count as effective uses of language (the statements of attainment set out for each level) are sufficiently vague to allow teachers considerable flexibility in devising their own assessments — though standard assessment tasks necessarily impose greater constraints. The illustrations I've provided of diversity in children's language suggest that it's important to take account of the context in which assessment takes place — 'context' being broadly defined to include features of the task children are engaged in, who they are working with and where they are working — in the classroom or elsewhere.

There is evidence from national monitoring that different children, and different groups of children, will perform better or worse on certain types of task. The Assessment of Performance Unit, which carried out national surveys of children's language performance during the late 1970s and 1980s, found a number of differences in girls' and boys' performance. For instance, in the 1988 survey of 11-year-old pupils' spoken language boys did better than girls on a task where they had to describe technically complex structures (two bridges); speculate and hypothesise about evidence from an experiment they had conducted; carry out a technological task (evaluating two can openers); plan an outing to an adventure centre; and argue a case relating to the building of a new motorway. Girls did better than boys on a task where they had to make up a story to explain events depicted in a picture (Gorman *et al.*, 1991).

As might be expected, the APU found an overall gender difference in tests of literacy: girls obtained significantly higher scores than boys in writing, and also tended to score more highly than boys in reading. But both girls' and boys' performances also differed on different tasks. The APU comment on reading:

> 'Performance is clearly affected by the interest pupils have in the topic or subject area, the focus of the questions they are asked to answer and the nature of the response required.' (Gorman *et al.*, 1991: 22)

And on writing:

> 'The findings from APU surveys confirm that ease or difficulty of writing is not a global characteristic, but something which can be significantly affected by various factors in the way a specific task is introduced, making some types of exposition easier than some types of narrative, and vice versa.' (Gorman *et al.*, 1991: 29–30)

While I've used gender as an example here, other aspects of children's social identity will be related to their experience of, and interest in, classroom activities — and so are likely to affect performance on different assessment tasks.

Children's language behaviour — particularly their spoken language — will also vary considerably depending on who they are working with. Young children may be more confident talking to an adult in pairs; a quiet child may work better in a group with the support of a close friend; a bilingual child may wish to work with another child who speaks the same language at home; for some activities children may prefer to work in single-sex groups. Children will also have experience of taking on different roles in discussion. For instance, there is some evidence that girls provide more 'conversational support' than boys — encouraging others to speak and acknowledging their contributions. It's often difficult to know what value to set on different types of contribution to a discussion. Some children's contributions will be highly visible. Other children, who appear quieter, may be helping to keep the talk running smoothly, or making a few well-timed contributions that change the course of the discussion. Because talk is, to a large extent, a group product, it's often hard — and it may not seem legitimate — to isolate the contributions of individual pupils. It's difficult, if not impossible, to separate judgements about children's language use from judgements about other things: the ways they relate to others in a group, or their knowledge of a particular topic. How important is it that children collaborate effectively in a group discussion, or that they use appropriate — maybe technical — vocabulary when they 'produce a range of non-chronological writing' (Writing, level 3)?

All these factors will affect the evidence children provide of their knowledge and ability, and trying out different types of assessment in different contexts may produce surprises. Sally Megram, a teacher in a combined (first and middle) school in Milton Keynes, suggests that observing children working outside the classroom can provide new information about those who are very quiet in more formal settings:

'... the children who are more willing to talk with you and share ideas with you can appear as the only ones who actually know what's going on, when quite often it's the quieter children [...] who are doing more thinking and linking more ideas in their own minds.' (Video interview for Open University course E623 *Assessment in the Primary Curriculum*)

Commenting on children's behaviour in different contexts, Patricia Murphy suggests that 'one should consider assessing children's powers of language in circumstances where they are at their best' (1991: 32). Clearly there is a balance to be struck between catching children 'at their best' and opening up new opportunities for children to work in a wider range of contexts, and on tasks they may find more challenging.

Teacher assessment cannot be separated from day-to-day classroom life. Children's perceptions of themselves as learners, their confidence and the evidence they provide of their ability will depend upon the overall ethos of the school and classroom — how work is routinely organised, how children are encouraged to approach their work and how they have learnt to relate to each other and the teacher. Sue Browne, a teacher from Brent, says of her own infant classroom:

'I think what's important ... is to establish in the classroom all the time a relationship with the children whereby you discuss ... their work and they tell you what they think about it — where they feel they might need help and where they think their particular strengths are — so that it becomes an ordinary part of the classroom situation.' (Video interview for Open University course E623 *Assessment in the Primary Classroom*)

Assessment formats

There is a range of ways in which speaking and listening, reading and writing may be assessed. I shall make a broad distinction here between 'objective' assessment, in which the assessment tasks, the particular aspects of language behaviour targeted, and the criteria by which they are to be evaluated are specified in advance and may be agreed by different assessors; and 'incidental' assessment, which is normally more open-ended and which tries to assess language 'on the hoof', as it occurs in real contexts. I think the distinction is useful though, in practice, it is not clear-cut — teachers may, for instance, pre-select certain tasks for assessment but try to assess children's performance in an open-ended impressionistic way. Either type of assessment, or a mixture of the two, may be used for teacher assessment within the national curriculum. A number of organisations (e.g. the National Association for the Teaching of English, the National Oracy Project) have advocated that teachers carry out incidental assessments of children's language, using an open-ended framework such as that devised for the Primary Language Record (ILEA/CLPE, 1988). Such records can be drawn on at the end of each key stage to allocate children to an appropriate level.

There are advantages and disadvantages attached to different assessment formats. From an equal opportunities point of view, 'objective' assessment has the advantage that it can be designed to be fairly reliable and less susceptible to the individual biases of different teachers. Gillian Brown and her associates, trying out objective assessment tasks with secondary school pupils, found that, when teachers used impression marking to grade children's spoken language, middle-class children were given higher marks than working-class children. This did not happen when teachers used an agreed set of criteria (Brown et al., 1984). On the other hand, 'objective' assessment may contain inbuilt biases (it may discriminate systematically against certain groups of children). And it cannot give a very full picture of what different children can do: the only aspects of children's language that are taken into account will be those that are specified by the assessment scheme.

'Incidental' assessment is better able to respond to diversity: teachers can sample children's language across a range of contexts as these occur in the classroom or elsewhere. They can record anything that seems relevant about children's language, rather than being bound by set criteria. Assessment is (necessarily) subjective, in that different teachers may legitimately note down different things about the same child. There is, however, a corresponding danger of bias. Teachers may see what they expect to see and systematically miss certain aspects of a child's language behaviour.

Making assessments of children's language immediately puts teachers in a position of power over children. It is normally teachers who decide what is important about a child's language — what deserves to be noted down and what doesn't. A number of assessment schemes — the Primary Language Record may be the best known — do try to include children's and parents' perceptions, for instance by holding discussions with children and parents and keeping a record of such discussions. As well as giving children and their parents a greater say in the assessment, this is likely to lead to a more complete picture of a child's language development and to help in planning appropriate language activities in the classroom. Sue Browne comments on her use of open notebooks to record children's achievements:

> 'It's important that [the children] feel they have some sense of owner-ship of the records — that they are their records about them and they can be proud of them and proud of their own achievements, and know that they're going to build on them.' (Video interview for Open University course E623 *Assessment in the Primary Curriculum*)

References

Brown, G., Anderson, A. H., Shillcock, R. and Yule, G. (1984) *Teaching Talk.* Cambridge: Cambridge University Press.

Department of Education and Science/Welsh Office (1989) *English for Ages 5-16* (The 'Cox Report'). London: HMSO.

Gorman, T. P., White, J., Brooks, G. and English, F. (1991) *Language for Learning: A summary report on the 1988 APU surveys of language performance.* Assessment Matters No. 4. London: School Examinations and Assessment Council.

Inner London Education Authority/Centre for Language in Primary Education (1988) *The Primary Language Record Teachers' Handbook.* London: ILEA/CLPE.

Minns, H. (1991) *Read It To Me Now! Learning at Home and at School.* London: Virago.

Murphy, P. (1991) Study Text for the Open University course E623 *Assessment in the Primary Curriculum.* Milton Keynes: Open University.

Savva, H. (1991) Bilingual by rights. *Language and Learning* 5, 6–10.

Shan, S-J (1990) Assessment by monolingual teachers of developing bilinguals at key stage 1. *Multicultural Teaching* 9(1), 16–20.

Part III:
Whole School

14 Starting Points

JACKIE HUGHES

When Jackie Hughes began a new job as head teacher in an inner city school in Birmingham, she had several aims: responding positively to cultural and linguistic diversity; challenging stereotypes based on gender and 'race'; developing better links with the local community; and involving parents more actively in their children's schooling. As a new head, however, a crucial issue was finding a starting point. Jackie decided to begin with her own practice and then to try involving other staff, parents and governors.

Introducing equal opportunities is never a straightforward matter. There may be conflicts of interest between different groups within the school; and there will be challenges from parents, pupils and staff. Jackie acknowledges some of the early problems she faced, and describes how she dealt with these. Her chapter shows how, gradually, a concern about equal opportunities began to inform all aspects of school and classroom life.

Introduction

Until 1989, I was deputy head and a class teacher in a large primary school in an outer ring area of Birmingham. The school had a commitment to equal opportunities, which pervaded all aspects of school life. I had become convinced that, for an equal opportunities policy to be effective, it needs to underpin whole school management, relationships between staff, pupils, parents and governors, classroom organisation and curriculum development. I was also convinced of the need to adopt a broad approach to equal opportunities: to pay attention to a combination of social factors, principally gender, 'race', social class and disability.

In January 1990 I took up a new post as head of St George's primary school, a mixed junior/infant school in the inner ring of Birmingham with approximately 214 pupils on roll. This chapter looks back over my first year at St George's. It is about how I am trying to promote equal opportunities

151

within the school — at first, in small ways, but eventually so as to involve all teachers, governors, pupils and parents.

St George's School

St George's school is in the parliamentary constituency of Ladywood. It is a Church of England aided primary school in an area of Birmingham which is ethnically and religiously diverse. The school population is culturally mixed: just over a third of the pupils are of white, European origin; others are either mixed race or of Pakistani and/or New Commonwealth origins. A substantial number of pupils in school therefore have their 'roots' in the Caribbean or Indian subcontinent as well as in Europe.

The main faiths represented in school are Christian (particularly from the black Pentecostal tradition), Muslim and Sikh plus a small number of Hindus, Rastafarians and Jehovah's Witnesses.

When I became head of St. George's there was a great deal of positive practice in the school. But there were also several aspects of school life that I felt needed further development. There was little representation of the diversity of the school's population in the form of display work around the school or in the type of curriculum resource materials generally available. Although the school had a large number of audio and visual aids principally for use with foundation subjects, history, geography, music, art/craft etc., not one celebrated the achievements of women or black people as important characters in world history, as discoverers or inventors, musicians or artists.

As I talked with pupils, staff, parents and governors it became apparent that there were several stereotypes about girls and boys, and black and white pupils: there was a feeling that boys, particularly those of Afro-Caribbean origin, represented the major discipline problems; that girls, particularly Asian girls, were more hard-working and well-behaved; and that Asians as a group had their own culture, different and separate from others in school. There was no attempt to respond positively to the diversity of cultures present in the school. There were few links between the school and its local community, and parents played little part in school life.

At the time, parents were expressing concern over 'standards' in school — they were concerned both about pupils' learning and their behaviour. Staff were sometimes negative about each other's performance as teachers, and there was little opportunity to provide mutual support. Pupils tended to be fractious with each other and the adults in 'authority' over them. Playground fights and disputes were numerous, as were complaints from parents about aggression in school. Staff meetings were often argumentative and accusatory, or quiet and resentful.

I felt these were issues we needed to tackle as a school, but many of them were sensitive. I needed to find a suitable way in to talking about these issues and bringing about change.

Small Beginnings

I knew of several resources we could draw on to increase children's motivation and broaden the range of practical activities and skills available to them: teaching packs, posters and books from organisations like Positive Image books or Handprint Publications in Handsworth; visitors from the West Midlands Arts Centre and the Commonwealth Institute; local theatre groups who could hold workshops with classes on African or Asian dance, stories and music-making. These activities could, I knew, be a vital spring-board for work in English, Maths and Science, but they hadn't so far been tried in St. George's. I wanted to explore these ideas with staff, but I also knew that if I tried to adopt a 'top down' approach to equal opportunities I would probably fail.

You may think a head is in a position of power in school, and to a great extent this is true. But it is not a position of unlimited power; a headteacher is dependent on others: pupils, parents, staff, governors, LEA, DFE, etc. Recent legislation, particularly the Education Reform Act, has increased the accountability of all teachers, heads included, so that this dependency has increased in some areas. For any school policy to be implemented successfully, to bring about real change, all these groups must agree that the policy is worthwhile — that it will bring about desired and agreed outcomes. Teamwork is essential. With the increase of parent and governor powers, and the increasing demands on teacher time and energy through national curriculum requirements, I knew that if equal opportunities was to be a meaningful model of management at St. George's, it had to be affirmed by everybody, not just myself, as a positive way forward for the school.

I began during my first two terms by simply talking generally about my own interest in equal opportunities whenever the chance arose. I purchased books (fiction and non-fiction), posters and teaching packs, that reflected positive images of women and girls, black people and disabled people. I chose material that I felt would counter stereotypes and broaden the range of images available to children: materials that portrayed girls in active rather than passive roles; that showed black people in history (Martin Luther King, Mary Seacole) and black scientists, inventors and politicians — both male and female; and that portrayed Africa and Asia as important areas of culture. I found a range of stories by Rachel Anderson about Jessy, a child with Down's Syndrome, that I felt would be a useful starting point in class discussions about disability.

I began to display these materials around school and talk about them in assemblies. My own teaching commitments were such that I had some contact with each class and so I began to read the stories and use the packs I had purchased, and display the childrens' work that arose out of this around the school. After a while, the staff, parents and children began to comment on these displays.

One or two teachers were apprehensive: they felt the new materials were too risky to use with children, and that they raised issues the teachers did not want to discuss. On the whole, however, responses were positive. Parents and governors were interested in the displays, and some staff began to use the new resources. Towards the end of my second term we introduced a new forecast document to help us plan our coverage of National Curriculum programmes of study and cross-curricular themes. For the first time, we incorporated equal opportunities into our formal curriculum planning.

Taking up the Challenge

While it's possible to do a certain amount of work on equal opportunities relatively informally, it helps to have structures to support and consolidate this work. We had already begun this with our forecast document. During the latter part of my first year several changes occurred which provided a broader base for equal opportunities. There were changes to the school's staffing structure, and governors and parents also began to play a greater part in school life.

Staff changes

As we neared the end of the summer term (my second term at St George's) it became apparent that there were going to be some staff vacancies for the following academic year. After discussion with the governing body and staff about the curriculum areas of responsibility for which we were going to advertise, I suggested that a commitment to equal opportunities be included in the wording of our advertisements. This received support from the governors, particularly two black parent governors, who had been especially pleased by the appearance of posters around school providing evidence of black achievements. They were keen that such initiatives should continue and be extended. By September 1990 our vacancies were filled by teachers with sound experience across the curriculum and with a proven commitment to fostering equal opportunities through cross-curricular approaches. This was a vital step forward. It meant we had more class teachers who were committed to using the curriculum to foster a positive self image among all pupils; to promoting relationships based on trust; and to co-operative patterns of learning and the peaceful resolution of conflict.

Involving governors

The two black parent governors were now beginning to play a much more active role on the governing body. The three of us were able to build up strong personal relationships, encourage one another, attend LEA-provided training sessions on equal opportunities and so keep the topic on the governing body's agenda. Support from the vice chair of the governors, a Baptist minister with a strong commitment to social justice, meant we were developing a caucus of people with an openly articulated concern for 'education for all'. The two black parent governors now began to view themselves as a resource. They were able to come into school frequently, and their involvement in classrooms (both offered to hear readers, help with PE and art and craft) meant that they felt valued and that their knowledge about black children was seen as important. They were keen that such initiatives should continue and be extended.

A parental questionnaire

We had begun to tackle discipline and classroom management as issues in school. After looking at the recommendations of the Elton Report, we decided to send a questionnaire to parents to ask for their impressions of the service the school provided. We included questions about our provision of equal opportunities in the curriculum, about classroom management and about whole school behavioural policies. Approximately 80% of parents replied and underachievement, particularly among black pupils, featured largely in their responses. Parents also raised concerns about discipline. On the positive side they appreciated our attempts to raise the profile of minority ethnic groups in school. Many felt the school had not done enough in the past to affirm the identity of black children and encourage them to succeed. Parents were also pleased that we were encouraging all groups in school to acknowledge their different cultures and backgrounds.

As a staff, we discussed parents' responses to the questionnaire. The need for sound classroom management techniques and a broad curriculum throughout the whole school was apparent. The deputy headteacher (the only male member of staff) attended a four-day course on behaviour management organised by a team of educational psychologists. This course further emphasised the use of the curriculum to affirm cultural backgrounds and foster a positive self image among all pupils. The deputy head played a strategic role in organising a meeting for parents, teachers and governors to discuss how we could work together to develop a whole school behavioural policy in which equal opportunities would play a fundamental part. This meeting gave parents a forum to discuss their expectations of teachers, and vice versa, so that we could share common strategies for pupil management.

Saturday schools

Several parents came into school to talk about their children attending black Saturday schools. The first parent to raise this issue was Marilyn, one of our lunch time supervisors. She mentioned someone I knew in Handsworth, who was involved in Saturday schools. She asked my opinion on the value of Saturday schools — would it be overloading her child, and would different teaching methods confuse him?

Marilyn felt her child was intelligent, but underachieving. She was anxious that he should not be seen as a problem because of this. She was reassured when I said I would be happy to liaise with a Saturday school if she chose to send her child to one, and that I thought it could have positive outcomes for her child to have contact with a black teacher: it would be a good role model for him. My main sadness was that she obviously perceived the school as not stimulating her child sufficiently and enabling him to realise his potential. That she should have to pay for his education to be supplemented seemed to me a gross example of inequality. It also raised the question about why so few black teachers are to be found in LEA schools. Marilyn and I discussed her worries about her child with his class teacher. We looked carefully at the programmes of work her child was being offered in school. This left Marilyn feeling very much happier. She is still thinking about the use of a Saturday school in the future if her child does not make the progress she expects, but for the present she is satisfied that the quality of teaching at St George's is improving and that this will obviously benefit him. I am convinced though, that Marilyn's dilemma about her child is just the tip of the iceberg, that many black parents share her concerns and that it is the school's duty to take these concerns on board by having much higher expectations of what black children can achieve.

A training scheme for parents

In June 1990 we introduced a parents' Employment Training scheme in child care. This was part of a community project to enable parents to receive training for future employment but it also involved them in the day-to-day life and organisation of the school. These parents are now so much a part of school life that under Local Management of Schools we hope to make them permanent. They work in a co-operative way with teachers and pupils, bringing an invaluable perspective to school life so that without them we would be impoverished.

Parents work alongside teachers. They hear readers, discuss the text with the child and ask questions about what happened and why. They take small groups for art and craft. They display work around school. They are currently helping with assessment — for instance, working with individual children using maths games to assess a child's mathematical knowledge. They have built up close relationships with the class teachers with whom they work and have developed considerable skill in designing language and maths activities for pupils. Class teachers used some of their class release time to help train parents, showing them different display techniques, planning work for children with parents, discussing intended outcomes etc. All parties — staff, parents and children — have benefited enormously from the Employment Training scheme.

Where We Are Now

We have now seen some reorganisation of the school's hierarchical structure. The appointment of new staff, particularly women in senior management positions, and the involvement of parents in school discussion and decision-making processes, has meant that equal opportunities are not just a matter of good classroom practice but of school organisation and management. The postholder for English has begun to lead the staff in examining reading materials and 'standards' in school. She has led staff meetings (traditionally this was the preserve of the head and deputy) and she has involved parents in piloting new books and in making decisions about purchasing.

As part of our staff development programme we have begun regular in-service training on gender issues and racial justice led by LEA advisers. We are now taking on board the implications of Birmingham LEA's equal opportunities policies. The school is taking part in a 'women of the future' project developed by the city's adviser for gender, and in a cross-curricular, multicultural project entitled 'The World Around Us'. This will culminate in a display of childrens' work at the city museum and art gallery. Standards of discipline are now improving. Display work around school is varied and reflects the diversity of the pupils. Perhaps most importantly, relationships in school are much warmer. We now photograph all aspects of school life and display this evidence of our children's achievements in prominent places around school to draw visitors' attention to the diversity of our school and community — a diversity of which we are very proud.

We still have a long way to go — we are trying to improve delivery of the National Curriculum, and like most schools we are grappling with

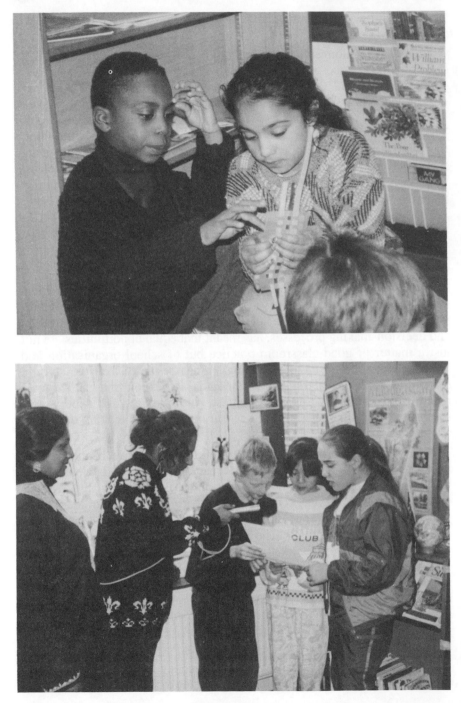

Photo upper left: Boys and girls at St George's are positively encouraged to work in partnership. Girls are encouraged to take a lead where possible.

Photo lower left: Outside visitors, particularly black people and women, representing good role models and talents are encouraged into school to work with children as often as possible. This group are learning broadcasting skills for a local community radio programme.

Photo above: Boys as well as girls are encouraged to take part in dance activities. This photograph shows a workshop organised by South Asian Arts Development, exploring the telling of traditional Indian tales through movement and dance.

assessment and record-keeping. We are tackling this through a system of increased planning, colleague support, and release of all postholders to work alongside class teachers to share expertise and improve the quality of teaching and learning.

As far as developing a written whole school equal opportunities policy is concerned — that is still to be done, as we wish any such document to be the product of parents, teachers, governors and if possible children working together. A written policy will still need to be subject to constant review so that the cycle of policy into practice and practice into policy will be ongoing.

Some Reflections

Introducing equal opportunities into the curriculum is far from plain sailing — it calls for commitment, risk taking, learning new approaches to both teaching and classroom organisation. Not all teachers are willing to take this on board or feel they are able to. This has been the case at St George's with one or two. Also, not all parents are supportive. One white parent objected very strongly to a class visit to Birmingham Central Mosque. She believed this would expose her child to beliefs and practices alien to her own culture and would therefore confuse her. The class teacher and I talked to the parent. We invited her to attend the visit and see that the staff at the mosque did not intend to 'indoctrinate' her child, but to explain something about Muslim belief and ceremony. The parent decided to let her child go. Equal opportunities teaching does mean teachers are challenged by both pupils and parents. It does not make for an easy life, but then neither does any area of teaching if we are committed to doing it to the best of our ability.

On looking back on my first year at St George's, I think it was right to begin with my own practice — with assemblies, my own teaching commitments, and the purchase of resources. It was also useful to involve those members of the governing body who were already aware and interested in equal opportunities issues. Appointing new staff has been a key factor, for no-one can carry out prolonged efforts alone. Now that we have a body of people committed to cooperative learning, issue based teaching and involving parents in decision making, the task is getting easier. Our big problem is lack of time because of the pressure to implement National Curriculum programmes of study, pupil assessment, and teacher appraisal. I am worried that equal opportunities will gradually be squeezed out of the curriculum altogether.

With hindsight it might have been better to confront issues such as underachievement as a whole staff rather than on an individual teacher and pupil basis. Perhaps we should also have tried to hammer something out on paper, however minimal, right from the beginning. I do feel though that our progress at St George's demonstrates a measure of success: the school is now a livelier, more stimulating environment; diversity has greater acknowledgement; and standards of teaching have been vastly improved. Where there are problems or difficulties these are there to be worked at. No school is ever perfect but a good school knows its limitations and weaknesses and works to improve upon them.

Resources

Some of the resources we have found useful in our work are:

(1) South Asian Arts Development, Midland Arts Centre, Cannon Hill Park, Birmingham B12 9QH. Tel. 021 440 4221 Ext. 206. Director Piali Ray.

(2) *Gender Differentiation in Infants Classes*. Equal opportunities Commission for Northern Ireland, 1987.

(3) *Changing Stories* and other publications of ILEA English Centre, Sutherland Street, London SW1.

(4) *Hidden Messages: Activities for Exploring Bias* 1986. Available from Development Education Centre, Selly Oak Colleges, Bristol Road, Birmingham B29 6LE.

(5) *Theme Work: A Global Perspective in the Primary Curriculum in the '90s*. 1991. Available from Development Education Centre, Selly Oak Colleges, Bristol Road, Birmingham B29 6LE.

(6) World Studies Publications (8–13). David Hicks and Miriam Steiner (eds). London: Oliver & Boyd, 1989.

(7) *Self Esteem: A Classroom Affair*. Michelle and Craig Barba. London: Harper & Row, 1989.

(8) *Changing Images: Anti-racist, Anti-sexist Drawings. Natalie Ninvalle, 1984. Sheba Feminist Publishers, 488 Kingsland Road, London E8.*

(9) Positive Image Books, Unit 1 Zair Works, Bishop Street, Birmingham 5.

(10) Handprint Publishers, 9 Key Hill Drive, Birmingham B18 5NY.

References

Anderson, R. (1990) *Best Friends*. London: A & C Black.
Anderson, R. and McNicholas, S. (1990) *Jessy Runs Away*. London: Young Lions.

Committee of Enquiry into Discipline in Schools (1989) *Discipline in Schools*. Report of the Committee of Enquiry chaired by Lord Elton (the Elton Report). London: HMSO.

15 Developing a Whole School Approach for Dealing with Bullying in the Primary School

CELESTINE KEISE

Bullying involves behaviour ranging from verbal abuse to serious physical injury, and in a few cases has resulted in the victim's death. It is basically an abuse of power, and that abuse can actually be assisted by school systems and structures. What can be done to reduce bullying, which research suggests may affect some 30% of primary school children? From her experience of in-service work with inner-city schools, Celestine Keise suggests a number of starting points:

How Significant is Bullying?

'Well you get it for being Jewish
And you get it for being black
Get it for being chicken
And you get it for fighting back
You get it for being big and fat
Get it for being small
Oh those who get it get it and get it
For any damn thing at all.'

           (Adrian Mitchell, 1984, 'Back in the Playground Blues')

'Bullying is the most malicious and malevolent form of deviant behaviour widely practised in our schools and yet it has received only scant attention from national and local authorities. It has failed to claim the attention of teachers' unions, our schools have given it low priority compared with disruptive behaviour and truancy, and finally it has been ignored by the educational research community.' (Tattum, 1989)

The reason for the focus today on bullying in our schools cannot be too heavily stressed. Bullying is very much an equal opportunities issue. Pupils who are bullied are being denied access to learning in the safe and caring environment to which they are legally entitled. The National Curriculum is an entitlement curriculum yet we know that the effects of bullying can make this meaningless for a bullied pupil who may be too frightened to participate in class and in some cases too terrified to attend school.

It is recognised that bullying is an abuse of power. Often our school structures and systems assist the bullies in their bullying behaviour, for example, when supervision is inadequate at breaktimes or when pupils are not reprimanded for name calling or hurtful teasing.

Several researchers have found that fear of being bullied is one of the main concerns voiced by primary children and their parents at the transfer to secondary school stage. The resulting pattern of absenteeism, truancy, illness, loss of confidence and self-esteem, suicide and murder, that can be the end result for the victim, has serious and obvious consequences for the victim's ability to learn and to achieve, for the bully's future social development (the bullying child frequently becomes the violent adult) and for the whole school environment. We need also to consider how to enable 'bystanders' to deal with what they see.

I became involved in anti-bullying work initially as an advisory teacher for gender equality with the Inner London Education Authority and subsequently in my role as Inspector for Gender Equality in an inner London borough. When working in both secondary and primary schools I have felt it important from the beginning to find ways to empower the staff (individually and collectively) within the schools to take the initiative forward into the classroom and into the wider school community. It is, therefore, important that teachers are given the time to explore and debate the issues and to reach a consensus of opinion on what bullying is and how to deal with it in their particular school.

In my role as inspector I am now able to provide schools with support from the Local Education Authority both in terms of policy and guidelines, borough-based training and financial assistance. The Local Education Authority context is also an effective means of sharing good practice and networking.

In this chapter I shall describe briefly some of the work in which I have been involved with inner London schools (pseudonymns are used for all schools and pupils referred to). I shall give details of an anti-bullying initiative in one particular primary school in the borough, Fernleigh Primary, which has dramatically changed the school's ethos and environment. I have found that similar issues crop up in relation to bullying at primary and at secondary level.

The last few years have seen an increase in interest in bullying in Britain from the media, researchers, the public at large and some local educational authorities. This has been mainly due to the horrific bullying attacks experienced by some pupils which have prompted relatives to speak out and Local Education Authorities to act. The two most publicised accounts are perhaps those centred around Mark Perry and Ahmed Ullah. Mark Perry's death, as a result of bullying, led his mother to establish the Anti-Bullying Campaign together with Kidscape in 1988. The death of Ahmed Ullah at Burnage High School in 1986 led to the extensive MacDonald Inquiry, a flurry of media attention, the anti anti-racist backlash from the Right and some action from Local Education Authorities to prevent the same thing happening in their schools (e.g. the Inner London Educational Authority in the particular brief that I was given). At the same time the Government Commissioned Elton Report on Discipline in Schools, published in 1989, emphasised the need for schools to recognise and deal with bullying and racial and sexual harassment (see Sections 65–7 of the report). Although Mark and Ahmed were both secondary school pupils, large-scale research in primary schools shows that 30% of children are involved, either as bullies or victims (Smith & Thompson, 1991).

However, a national anti-bullying campaign (as in Norway) has yet to take place in Britain. The government has only very recently decided to allocate funding to Sheffield University to carry out research specifically into bullying in schools. In the meantime it is left to individual schools and Local Education Authorities to take action.

Both Mark's and Ahmed's deaths had a racist dimension to them. Although racism is not always a factor in bullying it can be a significant one and one which is felt by the black community, as I write, to be on the increase. For instance, a pupil in the primary school where I have been recently working commented:

Lorna: Bullying is just one of the problems we need to solve. There is also racism. It's not just to one race. It's to all other race in the school. (Year 6 pupil (age 10))

We need to be aware of the differing experiences of harassment and bullying for black and white pupils, for working class and middle class pupils, and for girls and boys, in order to arrive at a clearer understanding of the dynamics at play and in an attempt to find effective strategies for bringing about change.

Part of my work with schools wishing to address bullying has been to develop with them their own individual working definition of bullying.

Most definitions, provided by research, acknowledge an imbalance of power and an abuse of power with the dominance of the powerless by the powerful. Bullying is seen as an act which is repeated over a period of time (though this is not always considered to be necessary) and one that can be physical, psychological or verbal in nature. Finally, it causes damage and distress to the victim. It is also recognised that a highly competitive sporting, academic or social school ethos can contribute to bullying as such an ethos causes feelings of inferiority and distress in those unable to live up to the rigorous demands that are set. Therefore, how we teach as well as what we teach is important.

What has become very clear in recent studies is that the incidence of bullying amongst girls can be as high as that amongst boys but because girls frequently bully in less overt ways their behaviour often goes unrecognised. This is poignantly seen in the following remark taken from an interview with the 10-year-old pupil at Fernleigh Primary School already quoted above:

Lorna: I didn't think it was bullying because when you're younger you don't really understand if it's bullying or not.

She wasn't being hit but the bully was certainly, through her ability to exclude Lorna and manipulate others in the friendship group, in a more powerful and therefore dangerous position. Also the pain, fear and shame Lorna experienced was possibly as intense as that experienced by a victim who has been physically bullied.

Lorna: I felt hurt, I felt like I sometimes wanted to cry, as I'm a very nervous person, and I get upset easily and picked on easily and sometimes I felt like not getting up in the morning and pretending I had a cold or something, as I didn't know what was going to happen during the day.

What Does Bullying Mean to Pupils?

My work with the Equal Opportunities Working Party at Lamont girls' school in the same inner London borough led to a half day's training session on bullying for the whole school staff — organised by members of the Equal Opportunities Working Party. As part of the follow-up, staff decided to devise a simple questionnaire about bullying, which all pupils were asked to complete. The staff found the girls more than willing to share their experiences. Pupils' responses were honest and revealing, and it was obvious that the lid had been lifted off something which was of deep concern to them.

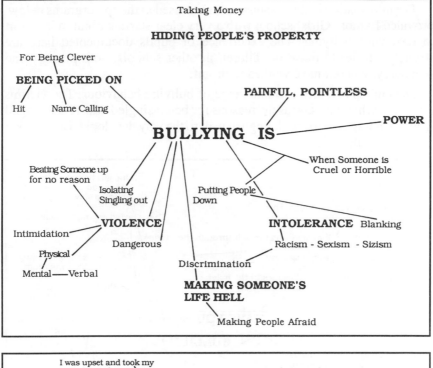

The information in the responses, summarised in the spidergrams below, provided Lamont Girls' school with a very clear starting point in its effort to deal with bullying. The experience of pupils documented here are strongly similar to those of children in other schools, both primary and secondary, where I have worked with staff.

The bullies revealed a whole range of bullying behaviour. The victims identified what they saw as the reasons for being singled out. These ranged from not being able to speak English well to the way they looked and spoke: the list is endless.

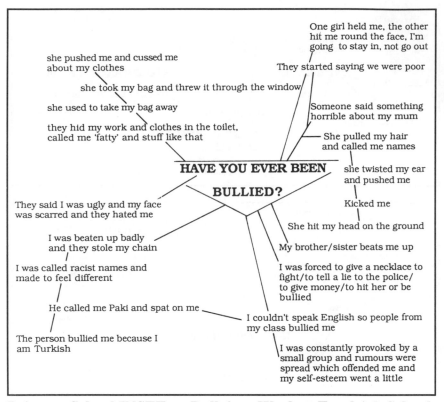

Primary School INSET on Bullying: Work at Fernleigh School

I was invited by the recently appointed headteacher of Fernleigh school to lead staff in two half-day in-service sessions on the theme of bullying. This had been identified as a serious problem within the school along with racial harassment and a high degree of violent and aggressive behaviour. Fernleigh is housed in a spacious Victorian triple decker building. The 200 pupils come mainly from a white, working class background but there are a significant number of black and ethnic minority pupils; many of these children are bilingual or speak three or more languages.

On her appointment to the school the headteacher was extremely concerned by the negative and aggressive ethos that she found. Pupils were frequently verbally abusive towards each other and towards staff. Physical aggression and bullying loomed large in playground behaviour and around the school generally. Furthermore, the head found that the staff seemed somewhat fatalistic about the children's behaviour and their own responses to it. It seemed to them that little could be done; that's how the children were and at best all they could do was to try and 'manage' the childrens' behaviour.

The head was very clear that what was urgently needed, if children were to learn and to achieve, was the creation of an ethos which 'should be caring, calm and patient'.

'Adults must be available to listen to children, and to give them time. All adults must set an example of mutual support, co-operation and respect for one another. There must be a policy of non-violence and non-aggression. Adults should not shout at or threaten children.' (Taken from the school's development plan, 1990)

The first INSET session

The first session took place at the beginning of the summer term. By the end of this session, awareness had been raised, a tentative definition of bullying had been developed and staff had identified possible strategies for dealing with bullying. These included, for example, the use of assemblies to raise the children's awareness and to talk about incidents; involving parents at an early stage by informing them of bullying behaviour which had involved their child; the logging of incidents in an incident book.

The session ended with staff identifying possible strategies which they wanted to discuss and develop in the second session, including:

- informing parents of the anti-bullying initiative;
- the setting up of an action group to take the initiative further;
- the use of bully courts (a strategy suggested by Kidscape which involves pupils directly in the resolution of bullying incidents);
- a school survey on bullying.

The second INSET session

The second session was held some six weeks later. On the basis of work in the first session we had drafted the following aims:

- developing strategies for involving the whole school (i.e. parents, children, teachers, governors, support and ancillary staff);
- developing preliminary whole school guidelines;
- addressing bullying through the curriculum (i.e. the national curriculum and the wider curriculum, organisational implications, resources etc.);
- using case studies to identify short and long term strategies;
- developing strategies for monitoring and evaluation (including performance indicators);
- identifying what is happening in the playground.

On reflection I was overly optimistic that all these could be addressed in a three hour session but we had a good try! Staff were divided into three groups and were asked, with the aid of prompt sheets provided by me, to focus specifically on issues around:

- developing guidelines for dealing with bullying incidents;
- addressing bullying through the curriculum;
- behaviour in the playground.

Staff were then asked to plan a course of action for each of these areas and to identify specifically:

- how they would involve pupils, parents, the staff, governors;
- how they would monitor and evaluate the targets set;
- what performance indicator they would use to establish whether the target had been met.

Finally, we examined a number of case studies on bullying. The importance of the use of case studies as part of a training session cannot be too heavily stressed. They allow participants to focus on the need to develop short term strategies and consider their immediate response to a real situation. Far too frequently we fail to respond appropriately/effectively when an incident occurs because we are unsure of the school's position or lack confidence in dealing with certain types of behaviour. I have found this to be particularly so for incidents of a sexist or racist nature.

For each case study participants were asked to identify what makes it a bullying or harassment incident and to decide on the short and long term strategies that need to be used in order to resolve the incident. Some people found it helpful to use role-play. Examples of two of the case studies are given below.

Case study A

As curriculum coordinator for science you are supporting a class teacher. At the start of the lesson a small boy, Michael, complains to his teacher that he has been hit by another boy in the playground. He adds that this same boy also waits for him at home time, calls him names and snatches his bag. His teacher tells him not to be such a wimp and to stand up for himself. In fact, the teacher taunts him in front of the other children saying 'who's a cry baby then?'

Case study B

A parent informs you that her daughter, Amina, who started school in September in year 5 has recently been very upset. Three girls in her class have been calling her names, telling her that she smells and that she should go back to where she came from. That same morning in your lesson with the group you notice the three girls pushing her while another grabs her bag and hold it at arms length.

Participants can obviously use incidents from their own schools as case studies.

Follow-up work

Following this session, the staff decided to use the remainder of the summer term to begin work on the playground, and to launch a whole school anti-bullying initiative at the start of the autumn term. The initiative would include:

(1)   Detailed sanctions for dealing with a range of incidents including the setting up of a break time detention for pupils involved in disruptive playground behaviour.

(2)   An incident logging book to be used by playground supervisors as well as teaching staff.

(3)   Assemblies to reward pupils for positive behaviour etc.

As part of the focus on the playground the staff agreed that for the remainder of the summer term they would spend ten minutes after each playtime talking through what had happened in the playground with children so that any incidents could be immediately identified and dealt with. By the end of the summer term there was whole staff agreement that anti-bullying and anti-harassment work would be identified as a target within the School Development Plan and would make up 25% of all staffing meeting time and INSET time in the next academic year. The teaching staff together with the headteacher used a staff meeting to brainstorm ideas for the playground (identified as the starting point for the project) and then used the outcomes of this brainstorm to plan a topic web for work in the first half of the autumn term. Part of the first INSET in September was used by staff to share their planning and to coordinate a whole school approach.

I visited the school some ten weeks into their autumn initiative and was amazed at the transformation that had already taken place. Classrooms and corridors were full of displays of pupils' work ranging from drawings showing 'how to say no', and 'what is bullying' to imaginary stories of ET visiting a school where bullying was rife. One story showed ET leaving because he was so upset by what he saw, but returning some time later to find a warm, supportive and caring environment and then deciding to stay! Assemblies were frequently used to remind children how to deal with bullying. The headteacher discussed the school's stand on bullying with all new children and their parents/guardians.

The headteacher informed me that several parents had commented on how much more welcoming and positive the atmosphere now was in the school. The incident log book was firmly established and being used by support staff and teaching staff alike. (A separate, brief training session had taken place between playground helpers and the headteacher.) All the children I spoke to were able to tell me about the school's strategies for dealing with bullying and commented positively on the changes they had noticed:

Sharina: We talk about how it feels to be bullied, and there was this board like showing what to say if someone comes and bullies you, like say 'go away, leave me alone, and stop bullying me', and once they don't leave you alone you tell the teacher.

Peter: There used to be a lot of bullying but since we had our new headteacher, a lot of it has gone.

Gary: There ain't a lot of bullying in the school now. There used to be a lot.

Gary: We get told off ... stay in for detention, stay in break times, write about why you bully and write to say sorry.

One very important aspect of the work being done is the recognition by the staff of the need to involve the pupils in the resolution of incidents.

Several staff had visited a primary school in a neighbouring borough which held regular 'bully courts' as suggested by 'Kidscape'. However, the staff at Fernleigh school had decided to adopt regular 'trust and tell' sessions in which children in each class together with the class teacher have a forum for raising concerns, and disputes which the whole class is then involved in resolving[1]. This is still very much at the experimental stage but staff and children are very enthusiastic about the idea.

The work in Fernleigh is by no means complete. The excitement of such an initiative is that it creates a climate of experimentation and transformation. The school is now focusing on increasing parental involvement in the initiative. Parents have already been informed by letter of the initiative and the logging of incidents has been an extremely effective way of detailing to parents their child's behaviour over a period of time. The school is now exploring with a local Theatre in Education group the possibility of a school production (with an anti-bullying theme) which will actively involve parents. It is hoped that this will also help the school to develop more positive relationships with some parents whose own bullying and aggressive behaviour and attitude towards the staff has been a cause for concern.

At the same time the school has also participated in a Local Education Authority anti-bullying initiative which I have developed to support the work in schools. This has involved the use of a self-defence and assertion trainer to work with teachers and pupils in their classrooms to develop strategies that can be used if one is being bullied. The work also involves looking at strategies for channelling aggressive, bullying behaviour into a more assertive and less damaging response. I have been able in my role as inspector to secure funding for this initiative in some 30 primary schools and to promote such initiatives with the full backing of the Education Department which recognises that harassment and bullying can have no part to play in a child's schooling if that child is to achieve her or his full learning potential.

The Way Forward

Schools working in this area have found that there is no one particular way of dealing with such a complex issue. Rather there needs to be an approach which constantly revisits the issue and which keeps it on the agenda supported by a range of strategies. Whole staff training, the setting up of an incident recording system, trust and tell sessions, working with parents, the use of Theatre in Education companies such as 'Neti Neti' or 'Pop Up' (borough-based Theatre in Education groups), the creation of a bully line (a pupil organised and run support network for pupils being bullied), including bullying as a topic within the curriculum, the use of literature and the use of assemblies are just some of the many initiatives that have been tried within schools. Bullies may always be with us but there is a great deal that can be done to minimise the existence of bullying and its effects.

Notes

1. See Claire (1991) in resource list for details about how these, and other safe forums for children to talk through conflict and personal issues, can be organised.

Resources (compiled by Hilary Claire and Celestine Keise)

General books and articles

Besag, V. (1989) *Bullies and Victims in Schools. Milton Keynes: Open University Press.*

Claire, H. (1991) *We Can Stop It! Whole School Approaches to Combat Bullying: A Handbook for Teachers.* Islington Safer Cities Project with Islington Education Authority (obtainable from Islington Education Authority).

Elliott, M. (ed.) (1991) *Bullying: A Practical Guide to Coping for Schools.* London: Longman.

Keise, C. (1992) *Sugar and Spice? Bullying in Single-sex Schools.* London: Trentham Books.

Roland, E. and Munthe, E. (eds) (1989) *Bullying: An International Perspective.* David Fulton Publishers, in association with the Professional Development Foundation.

Ross, C. and Ryan, A. (1990) *'Can I Stay in Today Miss?' Improving the School Playground.* London: Trentham Books.

Smith, P. and Thompson, D. (eds) (1991) *Practical Approaches to Bullying.* David Fulton.

Tattum, D. and Lane, D. (eds) (1989) *Bullying in Schools.* London: Trentham Books.

Tattum, D. and Herbert, G. (1990) *Bullying: A Positive Response: Advice for Parents, Governors and Staff in Schools.* Cardiff: SGIHE.

Books for pupils

Infants

Anderson, R. (1991) *Best Friends.* London: A & C Black.

A little girl with Down's syndrome is teased by her sister's friend, but everyone learns to deal with the unpleasantness in a positive way.

Elliott, M. (1991) *Feeling Happy, Feeling Safe.* London: Hodder and Stoughton.

A safety guide for young children. Includes notes for adults. Simple accessible stories with open-ended questions that will help a teacher raise issues for example who you feel safe with, what to do if you're bullied.

Glen, M. (1990) *Ruby.* London: Hutchinson.

Deals with teasing and name calling through the character of a soft toy who is 'different'.

Harvill, J. (1991) *Jamaica Tag-Along.* London: Mammoth/Octopus.

About being excluded.

Jenkin Pearce, S. (1991) *Rosie and the Pavement Bears.* London: Hutchinson.

.Rosie finds the courage to face her bullies with the help of her friends.

Junior

Blume, J. (1974) *Blubber.* London: Heinemann.

Grunsell, A. (1990) *Let's Talk About Bullying.* London: A & C Black.
Grunsell, A. (1990) *Let's Talk About Racism.* London: A & C Black.

Includes dealing with racist incidents and name calling.

Sanders, P. (1987) *Let's Talk About Feeling Safe.* London: A & C Black.

Includes dealing with taunting, bullying, sexism and racism.

Older pupils/teachers

Alcock, V. (1990) *The Trial of Anna Cotman.* London: Mammoth/Octopus.

About the power of the gang and the gang leader and the terror of the victim.

Atwood, M. (1990) *Cat's Eye.* London: Virago.

A woman has not really got over her experience of being bullied as a girl. Revealing about the causes and consequences for the bully as well as the victim's suffering.

Darke, M. (1989) *A Question of Courage.* London: Collins.

Set during the First World War, the sub-plot to this story about a young suffragette, is her brother's experience as a pacifist.

Organisations

Kidscape, 152 Buckingham Palace Road, London SW1W 9TR (071 730 3300).

Anti-Bullying Campaign (ABC), 18 Elmgate Gardens, Edgware, Middlesex HA8 9RT (081 906 3804).

16 Parents and Equal Opportunities

ANN WATSON

This chapter describes a school where parents are involved in every aspect of school life; they sign up for lunch, are timetabled to use apparatus with toddlers in the hall, and spent £2,000 in six months at the school bookshop. It is not a school for the children of middle-class professionals, however, but sits on the edge of a northern council estate where there is poverty in many families. Ann Watson, deputy head, explains how a commitment to parental involvement and to equal opportunities have sustained and supported each other in the work of the school over the past eleven years.

Introduction

I work in a Bradford First School. It is not a grimy, poky Victorian building but is flat roofed and spacious, looking like a liner that has got stranded on a hillside. It was built in 1960 as an infant and junior school which means that we have two of everything, including two large halls, and lots of space. We also have a large playground with trees and a beautiful grassy slope. From our windows we look on to acres of council house flats and houses with Bradford way over in the distance. We have three hundred children aged 4–9 (including those in the nursery) at the moment and only five are from ethnic minority groups.

Snapshot: Tuesday Morning

As you come in the front entrance you see a small parents' waiting area all done out in pale grey and red like a superior airport lounge. Gena, a classroom assistant and governor, chose the furnishings and set up the area. It has albums of photos of school life, an information board, photos of school staff — teaching and non-teaching — and a pay-phone booth.

176

In her office the headteacher, Pam, is talking to a new parent, going through our school booklet. The school secretary Kathy, always frantically busy, still has time to reassure a worried parent. If you turn right, you walk through the halls to the terrapin labelled Family Room, where a few parents are chatting over a cup of tea. Further across the playground is the nursery. Here a workshop system is set up and each area has explanations of the value of the activities, using mostly photos of the children.

Back in the main school again you can come into the Parent and Toddler Room — organised mainly by parents Val, Bev and Ann. You may notice that classroom doors have a Welcome sign with photos of staff and lists — 'When would you like to chat about your child? Please let me know'. There are notice boards and displays of the children's work specifically aimed at parents. There are school dinner menus (parents can stay to dinner if they book). There will probably be displays which indicate our approach to race and gender, for instance in a display about wood there will be photos of Linda, our nursery nurse, wielding her hammer. There is bound to be some information about books — something about some wonderful new books in our bookshop, or a newspaper clipping about ours being one of the most successful bookshops in the country! Nearly £2000 was spent on books in six months. In most classrooms there will be several adults — they will be teachers, nursery nurses, classroom assistants and a few parents (only a few have the time or the inclination to do this unpaid work on a regular basis).

In the staffroom there is a small group of mothers sewing in a craft group — set-up and run by Gena again. In another area Maureen, the Special Needs Coordinator, is talking to D, a single father about his six-year-old son P. There are difficulties about P coming to school on his own. His dad can't manage to bring him. Perhaps we can help.

On the way back you bump into two women who are collecting items of clothing for J, who has recently had a fire in her flat. Jean, the liaison teacher comes in the door with M, whose face looks bruised. They are discussing what happened last night. M would like to leave her partner but she hasn't decided where to go.

In the staffroom at playtime it is hard to tell who everyone is — to pick out the parents, teachers, Educational Welfare Officer, nursery nurses and classroom assistants.

Looking Back

I am sure many teachers will recognise this picture. Many first schools have close links with parents. The schools are accessible and they usually provide a pleasant place to meet. Teachers welcome extra help, especially with fund raising. Our involvement is extensive and has been for many years. A new headteacher, who is dynamic and committed, must have been the starting point. Another strong influence has been the way a commitment to parental involvement and equal opportunities sustain and support each other. Indeed, how can you separate them? If you care about opportunities for children, both girls and boys, you do for adults also. If you really think of parents as partners in their children's education then you must share ideas about the particular experiences of boys and girls.

From amongst the fluctuations of school life I have selected some milestones which may be useful for the reader (see diagram oppposite).

Equal Opportunities Work with the Children

Some years ago our approach to racism became an integral part of school life and now the same is happening with gender. Appointing an equal opportunities post resulted in many changes: what had been implicit for some of us became explicit for all. Ruth is refreshingly assertive. She started a programme of INSET for staff and, with the language coordinator, reformed our books selection procedures. The school library now has a special gender section with many stories about strong females. There are also many school made books. 'What do boys at Ley Top like to do?', 'What do girls at Ley Top like to do?', 'Wendy's motorbike', 'Our postwoman'. 'Mrs Moran builds a patio'. In the staffroom there is a new category in the staff library and on our noticeboard. As in most schools our registers are not separated for boys/girls. Neither are children expected to line up separately.

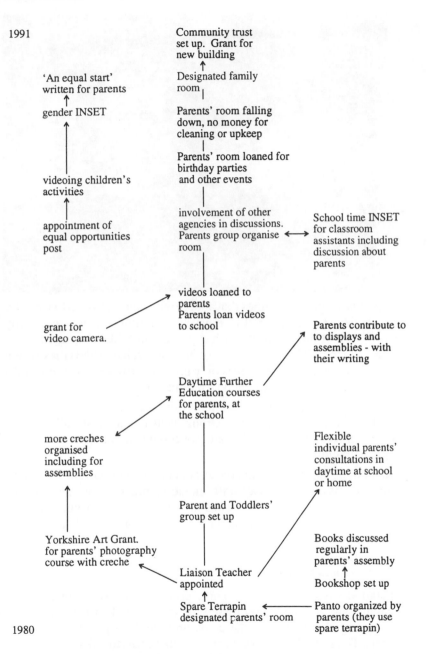

1991

Community trust
set up. Grant for
new building
↑
'An equal start'   Designated family
written for parents   room
↑ |
gender INSET   Parents' room falling
                          down, no money for
                          cleaning or upkeep
                               |
                          Parents' room loaned for
                          birthday parties
                          and other events
videoing children's |
activities   involvement of other
↑   agencies in discussions.   School time INSET
appointment of   Parents group organise ←→ for classroom
equal opportunities   room   assistants including
post   discussion about
                                                       parents

                          videos loaned to
                          parents
                          Parents loan videos   Parents contribute to
grant for   to school   to displays and
video camera.   assemblies - with
                                                        their writing

                          Daytime Further
                          Education courses
                          for parents, at
                          the school

more creches   Flexible
organised   individual parents'
including for   consultations in
assemblies   daytime at school
↑   or home

                          Parent and Toddlers'
                          group set up
Yorkshire Art Grant.   Books discussed
for parents' photography   regularly in
course with creche   parents' assembly
                          Liaison Teacher   ↑
                          appointed   Bookshop set up
                          ↑
                          Spare Terrapin   ←─── Panto organized by
1980   designated parents' room   parents (they use
                                                      spare terrapin)

Parental involvement in the school, 1980–91

Perhaps it is a sign of the times that about eighteen months ago Ruth took the school science post, instead of equal opportunities. This was mainly because of promotion prospects. It has proved an added bonus in some ways. For instance, she made a video of her class science activities which showed clearly her approach to girls only groups. Now she has produced a booklet for parents to borrow called 'An Equal Start'.

Our previous special needs coordinator introduced a policy to support quiet, withdrawn children. We take strong measures against bullying and support and advise mothers who are concerned about their children's aggressive behaviour.

Curriculum policies all contain discussion of equal opportunities issues. Working in teams encourages all staff, including nursery nurses and classroom assistants, to reflect these issues in their planning. It goes without saying that we also try to involve parents as directly as possible as you can see in the following ideas.

Project on skills and hobbies

This started small and grew into epic proportions, involving children, staff, parents, and anyone who crossed the threshold. It was a wonderful way of learning about skills in the community and for promoting certain role models. The school photographer and dentist came to talk to us. Wendy, the nursery nurse brought her powerful motorbike and a brave teacher took on Chantelle's mum at wrestling. We met a skin diver and one of the most amazing events was when glamorous Diane parked her car transporter lorry outside the school gates. We also celebrated traditional skills, emphasising the high quality of skill and training involved. There was Jill, the mum who designed and made wonderful knitwear, and the school secretary who amazed the children with her shorthand skills.

Project on food

We saw this project as a good opportunity to emphasise the pleasure and learning in preparing and serving food — for both boys and girls.

Some children were taken to a cafe where they were allowed to observe in the kitchen area. Back at school a cafe was set up where boys, dressed in chefs' outfits, served tea to parents as they came to collect their children. Boys were also involved in preparing and serving Asian and Yorkshire food for a teacher's lunchtime function.

Jean, the cook, talked about her job in assembly, emphasising her training and the bookkeeping and managerial aspects. She allowed small groups to visit the kitchen. We made a video of Debbie, the nursery nurse, in a baking session with five-year-olds and used it to show classroom assistants and parents how her skills made it a rewarding learning experience for those children.

A project in child care: Looking after babies

A teacher took a small group on a visit to a nearby clinic. The children, boys and girls, took photos of the baby weighing and talked to the nurses. Then they went into the doctor's room where Doctor Ansarai talked about her job. The children wrote about their experience and mounted the photos for display in the clinic. They did an improvised play for the school, *At the Clinic*. A parent, who is a governor chairperson, came to talk to her son's class about her job as sister in a premature baby ward, wearing her uniform and showing the tiny tubes and clothes. This was so successful that she spoke in assembly also and an entrance display was created. Care was taken to emphasise the responsibility of her job: that she was in charge of other nurses also. The fact that she is black was an added bonus for us.

A mother brought her baby into class for a bathing session. A single father talked about his most important job — looking after his children. A book was made about this. We also made a book about favourite dolls, with pictures of boys as well as girls holding dolls or cuddly toys.

Some other ideas in brief

- Mothers taking a family assembly about their *Return to Learn* work.
- Display of prizes: this resulted in a large collection of certificates from adults and children; everything from swimming to fishing. Medals and cups on display caused us some concern but nothing went missing.
- Asian girls from a nearby upper school worked with groups of children on a simple play. Our children went to their school where the girls videoed a performance. As with other videos, this was borrowed by parents.

Ways and Means: Keeping Parental Involvement on the Agenda

Looking back, some of our work appears haphazard as we sought to meet the demands of the time with an appropriate (and sometimes extemporised) solution or response, with the resources at the time and our own developing awareness. We have had many awful failures: sessions on maths and computers with only three parents — a terrible shuffling and early walk out in assemblies when we were trying to make educational points. 'Educating' parents never seemed to work, and perhaps they can best find out about such things working alongside children in the classroom. However, from considering these failures and successes I have been able to glean some lasting structures or principles which I think encourage positive growth.

Continuous dialogue between staff and individual parents

There is a formal system whereby, throughout the year, individual parents can choose a convenient time to chat to staff — usually when they collect their children. In many cases the child is involved in the discussion. Teachers are expected to make notes of significant conversations. There is also a rapport between most staff and parents that allows for an everyday exchange. The headteacher and liaison teacher are very accessible and the special needs coordinator spends a great deal of her time talking with families.

The headteacher talks to all new parents and discusses our policies including those on race and gender. Perhaps a creative approach to showing parents what we do arises from a yearning for an occasional pat on the back amidst a welter of bad press. At any rate, like many schools today, we do tend to say, 'that was good — how can we tell parents about it?'. Most parents know they can borrow our homemade videos and expect to see information for them on our walls and notice boards.

System of INSET in school time where most adults are considered

We work with outside agencies like the Further Education college and the RSPCC which we invited to put on various short courses during the day, such as drug abuse, child care, assertiveness training and word processing. When a group of parents took over organisation of the parents' room (see time-line), they planned and organised these activities, in collaboration with the school. Jean the liaison teacher's role was crucial here, as in all the work developing relationships with parents.

We find it very valuable to release classroom assistants every week for discussion/training with a senior staff member. We have had a similar programme with nursery nurses — but feel it more appropriate to involve them in teacher INSET.

Flexible approach to the use of space

We are lucky enough to have extra space and expect it to be used in school time — not just by staff and children — but by parents and outside agencies. For instance, the Parent and Toddler group, run by parents, are timetabled to use a hall.

We see parents as an important resource for children's learning

We get to know the skills of parents. The liaison teacher records useful information and can often suggest someone who will take small groups, talk in assembly or lend a special video: if she doesn't know then one of the dinner ladies is sure to. We have sung songs composed by parents, displayed many of their poems and pictures, and applauded at their pantomimes.

We have a support system for parents and staff

Virtually all the children in our school live in the surrounding council estate and there is poverty in many families. There is lack of support for women in particular. As I'm sure you realise, this problem doesn't only arise with single mothers. Some with partners are actually struggling on their own, deprived of money and abused.

Like many schools, we respond to these situations. It may be a case of involving other agencies. Often another parent can help. As one parent wrote 'If it had not been for the parents' room as a place where you can discuss problems and know you are not the only one — things would have been more difficult. ... And it is good to help each other ... like the time a women came in in a poor state. She was too scared to go back home and I spent all that day with her'.

Staff need support also; among other things, in meeting the demands of empowering others. Working in teams provides a supportive framework, and reviewing sessions with the headteacher are helpful. Also there is a feeling of empathy amongst many adults: and as we are mainly a female establishment (nearly all the parents we meet are mothers) it is an empathy amongst women that is encouraged to flourish.

Conclusion

Some of what has happened over several years at our school shows that we feel that a belief in equal opportunities must also mean extensive parental involvement. This is not an easy option and often we feel as if we are walking uphill in deep snow while being bombarded with snowballs.

When I think of rewards and benefits I am again reminded of the need for more precise evaluation. We *do* have one of the most successful bookshops in the country, with about £3000 a year spent by parents, many on very low income. The children bring their ten pences and buy stamps towards that beautiful new book. Their parents are often involved in choosing it. In recent testing of the 9-year-olds we can see an improvement in reading ability and much more interest in books. We are sure this is a reflection of parental interest.

We notice that certain shy girls are developing more confidence. And the 9-year-old boys: is it an illusion or do they seem more caring and sensitive than the 9-year-old boys of five years ago? We need to work out ways of evaluating our progress. It is not enough to be sometimes bathed in the warm glow of mutual support.

Our policies allow for this support; they also allow for considerable stress. If you empower others you have to learn how to cope with the inevitable demands of others' arguments and feelings. And times are already stressful for staff. We have learnt to express our fears and worries more openly to some parents, particularly, of course, to our governors. When we went to the Town Hall to demonstrate about staffing cuts, some parents hired a coach to come with us. And then, along with the traumas of Local Financial Management of Schools, there come more creative ideas about using money. We can actually pay one of our fathers to play the piano for us sometimes.

A new generation of assertive young women in school have stopped us tiptoing too sensitively around gender issues. The national curriculum *does* include passages about gender and race which set a seal of approval for parents. All political parties express a belief in parental involvement, and the significance of science and technology for girls. The future looks quite exciting.

17 An Equal Hierarchy

PETE SANDERS

Pete Sanders is head of a primary school in London. His commitment to equal opportunities is reflected in the way his school is organised and run to ensure that the whole staff share goals and personally experience good practice. While acknowledging his ultimate responsibility as head, he has set up structures — which he explains and describes in some detail — to involve everyone in decision-making.

Introduction

A school is not only an institution to which children come to learn. It is a learning place for everybody within it. In considering the development of children, it is imperative to consider staff development, by which I mean the whole school staff — teachers, helpers, schoolkeeper, nursery nurses, lunchtime supervisors, ancillary workers, students, etc. It is of little use to advocate respect for others amongst children, if this is not apparent amongst all the workers within the institution.

This was uppermost in my mind when I became a headteacher. My most daunting realisation, however, was that all the research was correct! The single most important aspect in the success or failure of a school is its leadership, and the style of leadership which one adopts will directly determine the ethos of the organisation. Yet management does not take place in a vacuum, and whilst I acknowledged the benefits of theoretical models of management, I knew that a manager inherits all kinds of situations within an institution — different power bases, inequality of experiences and opportunities, overt and covert conflicts, and so on. These need to be assessed in order to determine strategies to move forward.

Schools are structured organisations, and reflect the way in which the majority of our society is organised. Since I firmly believe that management is of paramount importance, I do not believe that a totally non-hierarchical school would be practical or achievable. I do, however, believe that equality of opportunity for all is essential to the well-being of any institution. For this reason I set out to try to introduce a model of management which would promote this equality, and be as non-hierarchical as possible. Within a school people have, or are perceived to have, different statuses, which are based on factors such as roles, experience, gender, length of time at the school, race, incentive allowances etc. A non-hierarchical model of management attempts to create a school ethos in which all staff, whilst they may not be equal in terms of job title, are equally valued, have equality of opportunity, equality of access to decision-making and information within the school, and space for issues to be aired and addressed.

I became aware very quickly of the need to be clear about my vision of education and to transmit this unambiguously. However, coming as I did from a health education background, I know that knowledge alone is not enough to effect change. To make choices which are right for us, we need to have a sense of self-esteem, a respect for others and a feeling that we are sufficiently in control of our own lives to achieve the outcomes of decisions which we make. In working with children on health issues, it was clear to me that a methodology which used active learning and group work was essential. Self-esteem is not developed through 'chalk-and-talk' sessions. I set out to translate this model into a whole school approach. This chapter will describe that approach, discuss its advantages and disadvantages and some of the outcomes. I hope to show that this kind of proactive management style can help to offset many problems before they become crises.

Developing the Team

In working towards an ethos which encourages equality of opportunity a real understanding of the true nature of teamwork is essential. Such an ethos is not created by individuals alone. People often talk about 'the team' when what they mean is a group of people who happen to be working together. Research has shown that children who are referred to as doing 'group work' are often actually engaged in carrying out individual tasks within a small group setting, with no real group objective (Galton & Simon, 1980). In the same way, the staff of a school is not automatically a team, simply because its members are carrying out similar tasks in the same institution.

In truth there is no easy way to describe what makes a group of people work effectively as a team. However, a recognition by all group members of three basic elements is essential:

- Tasks must have clearly understood objectives.
- Individuals within the group have their own needs and wants.
- The needs of the team as a whole must be met and maintained.

In developing teamwork, it is necessary to set up structures which will allow all workers to have a sense of purpose, an overview of the school, and a sense of ownership within the context of the whole school. Equality is both implicit and explicit in such a climate, and by setting up these structures, any issues which may arise have a forum for expression. The following are amongst the most important structures which I set up.

Communication

It may seem obvious to say that a good communication system is essential to the effective working of an institution, but this is all too often overlooked. Ways in which a team communicates must not only be in place, but also explicit and understood by all concerned. I worked out a pattern of communication methods, which was published to all members of staff. This was then revised and agreed as a whole group. As a new headteacher, I felt it important that effective communication links be set up as quickly as possible. To this end, I had to take into consideration my desire that as far as possible the group generated and owned the school's systems and balance this against the time necessary to achieve this. Whilst the manner in which we arrived at our agreed policy did not in this case present any problems, in retrospect, I feel that these procedures could have been established by the whole staff. The kinds of questions which would be asked to do this might be:

Who needs to communicate with whom?

What are the best ways to go about this?

What sort of frequency of communication is appropriate?

How will others be informed about the outcomes?

This list I devised was, however, presented to staff for comment and revision, and our final list of communication routes was as follows:

Weekly diary in administration area

Pigeon holes in administration area

Noticeboard of forthcoming events in administration area

Noticeboard of daily events in staff room.

Daily meetings for:

Headteacher/Deputy Headteacher.

Weekly meetings for:

Induction

Section 11

Headteacher/Schoolkeeper

Midday Supervisors

Infant/Early Years Department

Junior Department

School's Council.

Fortnightly meetings for:

Curriculum Development

Curriculum Coordinators

Helpers

School business.

Monthly meetings for:

Headteacher/Secretary (formal).

Half-termly meetings for:

Early warning meeting (to identify children with possible special educational needs)

Parent Governors/Headteacher.

Termly meetings for:

Governors

Finance committee.

Users of the building

Health and Safety.

Meetings

As you can see from the above list, the most important and frequent method of communication was through a pattern of meetings. Some of these meetings were already in place; others were new. A few people admitted initially to feeling a little daunted by the number of meetings. I explained my reasons for wanting these and stressed that each one was significant and would have its own very specific aims. No meeting would be held simply for the sake of it. It was very important to be clear about this. In fact, once the pattern was implemented, several staff commented how much more involved they felt in what was happening, both with the curriculum and the life of the school itself.

In an attempt to avoid ambiguity and assumptions, and to allow everyone to have a voice, I used active learning methods at most staff meetings from the outset. Whilst the majority of staff were used to working in this way during INSET days, they had also had experience of poor facilitators, which had influenced their opinion of active learning. Therefore it took several meetings for the staff to realise that it does work, when done properly. It was also important for me to convey my own confidence and belief in this methodology.

All aims were made explicit. For business meetings, the agenda was posted for everyone to see. For curriculum meetings, the aims would be decided by the person leading the meeting, and were usually very broad to allow discussion and negotiation (e.g. 'To develop our equal opportunities policy'). The purpose of every activity was declared and individuals were grouped in different ways, so that people who would not normally work together had the chance to do so. It also helped to avoid domination of the meeting by any individual, since all participants were given opportunities to feed back to the group.

For some meetings we had a 'rotating' chair, which meant that different people led the meeting. This was not only a useful way of building staff confidence and morale, but also put into practice my belief that staff should have ownership of the meeting. If people were uncomfortable about leading a meeting alone, there was the opportunity to work as a pair. It must be said that it was not compulsory for anyone to assume the role of facilitator. One member of staff felt unable to lead a meeting at all, and never did. Others were nervous but determined to 'have a go'. For most the experience was completely new. It was therefore very important to offer support and I made certain that I was available for anyone who wanted help with planning, or who needed advice about the appropriateness of activities etc. It was also vital that there was always a forum to evaluate how the sessions went.

In practice, the rotating chair meant that the quality of the leadership of the meetings varied quite considerably. Some people found it a natural role for them and were good at it. Others found it problematic. I feel, however, that it was an invaluable way of promoting staff development, both personally and professionally.

Wherever possible, we met together as a whole staff. This was quite often difficult, since teaching and non-teaching staff worked to different schedules. Naturally I seized every opportunity, such as election days, when the school was used for polling, to bring the whole team together. Such days involved a great deal of team building and team maintenance activities.

I have included below an example of the way in which I planned meetings. This is part of one of our INSET days on playground development.

This is still the format I use today, and I have found it extremely effective. Two points deserve special mention: I believe it is important to allow time at every meeting to acknowledge that people usually arrive at a meeting with much more on their minds than the business at hand! Giving a chance for this to be expressed means that people can then devote their energies

Purpose of every activity declared. ↙

224

TIME	ACTIVITY	PURPOSE	GROUPING	MATERIAL
1.00	All change	To regroup	WG	
1.05	In pairs: Talk about a playground you remember best. What did you like about it? What didn't you like?	To share experiences of playgrounds.	2s	
1.15	Feedback	To share ideas	WG	(whole group)
1.20	In groups of 5/6: List what is happening in our playground. Negative and positive aspects. Which of these have positive spin-offs in the classroom? Which have negative?	To analyse playground activities and evaluate them.	5/6	Paper
1.35	Feedback	To share ideas	WG	
1.45	Brainstorm: What are our aims in developing the outdoor learning environment?	To list aims of developing the outdoor learning environment.	WG	
1.50	Diamond Nines	To prioritise aims.	Alone/ WG	Statements Envelopes
2.10	Feedback	To share ideas	WG	
	Who might be involved in developing the playground.	To list potential community/agency links.	WG	
	What are the advantages/ disadvantages of involving others?	To identify benefits and possible problem areas.	WG	
2.25	Slide presentation.	To give practical examples of outdoor learning environment development.	WG	Projector
3.25	Graffiti wall	Evaluation	WG	
3.30	CLOSE			

Handwritten annotations:

Regroup after lunch when people tend to sit with friends. Energises group. (next to 1.00)

Feedback + debrief at all stages of the session. (next to 1.15/1.20)

working in different sized groups and allowing personal reflection time. → (next to GROUPING)

Each group member is given 9 statements to prioritise. Then join with other member to compare and discuss "diamonds" to try and reach a consensus. (next to 1.50)

Evaluation of each session is very important for group members and facilitator.
Here each group member writes down their feelings about the session on a small piece of paper, which is then attached to a larger sheet to make a "wall" and posted for all to see.

more fully to the purpose of the meeting itself. Evaluation is also of paramount importance. However immediate evaluations are sometimes less useful than more leisurely reflection on good and bad points and what one has learned. The true evaluation is whether what is decided in a meeting is translated to the classroom.

To ensure that primary school workers had an overview of the school, the meetings were structured so that the group itself identified areas that needed to be addressed. For example, when considering the content of our Institutional Development Plan, we met as a whole teaching staff group to identify what needed to be included, by brainstorming our ideas. We then formulated a checklist from the identified areas and worked in small groups to rate each area on a 1–5 scale, with 1 indicating a policy in place and 5 indicating that a policy needed to be developed. Thus, step by step, areas were prioritised.

We used an open agenda for meetings, which took the simple form of a book in which members of staff could write in points they would like to raise at specific meetings. Naturally, this self-agenda model tends to mean that more issues are on an agenda than can comfortably be addressed in the course of the meeting. For this reason a degree of prioritisation has to be undertaken. In this case, it was agreed by the whole staff that I should prioritise the content of the meeting from the open agenda. I also realised that it was important that we all had time to consider issues. Therefore we agreed to signal issues which were not to be discussed immediately, but which would be raised at a future meeting, once we had had time to formulate our ideas and opinions. On the other hand, people often had something they wanted to raise under 'Any Other Business'. Having noticed that this sometimes meant they were distracted throughout the rest of the meeting, we sometimes had 'Any Other Business' at the start of the meeting.

Having a model which used teamwork to reach decisions was also important when matters arose which were potentially difficult. For instance, when the time came to allocate incentive allowances, this was put to the group. People were asked to prioritise the needs of the school and generate a list of how they thought the allowances should be allocated. These lists were then considered by both myself and the deputy head and together we made the final allocations. In this way, even though the final decision is made by Senior Management, staff make a significant contribution and their feelings and priorities are taken into account.

Groundrules

At our first meeting as a group we generated a list of working groundrules for the team. This was not an arbitrary list of dos and don'ts, but an agreed record of principles to which we agreed to be bound. Initially, we brain-stormed suggested groundrules, then worked in small groups to finalise them. Below is part of the list of groundrules we generated:

Confidentiality

Staying on task

The right to challenge

Commitment to outcomes

Reaching consensus, even if this means voting

No racist/sexist comments

No smoking in meetings

Giving time and space to express ideas

Allowing everyone to contribute

Having time to reflect.

As you can see, many of these address equality issues directly. Having formalised groundrules was invaluable in giving people a legitimate way to challenge statements or behaviours which they felt were unacceptable. Of course, this does not always happen instantaneously. I was interested to see, however, how, after several meetings together, people became more comfortable about expressing their feelings. On one occasion a male member of staff was challenged about dominating certain meetings. This was obviously something which had been troubling other members of staff for some time. Once the issue was made overt, backed by the groundrules, it became easier to look at the problem and be positive in resolving it without recrimination.

We made certain that groundrules were revisited from time to time, in order that everyone remained aware of them, and to revise them if necess-ary. They became part of the contract we made as a whole school staff, and were integrated into job descriptions.

Equal opportunities policy

It may seem strange that a chapter devoted to promoting equality of opportunity amongst staff members does not lead with the importance of an equal opportunities policy. My reasons for this are quite simple. I believe that for any policy to be effective, people have to have a commitment to its implementation. I further believe that this will not happen unless people are consulted at all stages of the development of that policy, and feel that they have ownership. In order to agree a policy in this way, the kinds of structures I have described have to be in place. It is imperative that an equal opportunities policy (or any other school policy) is not simply a document setting out a series of desired aims, but a 'living' part of the whole school ethos. This is why I feel that team building to create a climate of trust and respect is vital.

The school already had a policy for equal opportunities, and because I wanted this to be current and active, we undertook a review of the policy. To do this, we first worked as a group and wrote down what we thought the existing policy was. We then compared our perceptions with the policy document. In this way, we were able to use the two sources to develop a new draft policy. We then worked in small groups to refine and finalise an agreed policy.

As well as the policy itself, we also looked at strategies for its maintenance. As with all policies in the school, it was important that we presented a consistent approach to its implementation. All members of staff were empowered to challenge any behaviour which was contrary to the policy, either on the part of children or adults. The way in which this was done was also important. Since we had developed an ethos which respected other people, we found that challenges could be made in a non-threatening way. After all, we had agreed as a staff that when dealing with certain behaviours by children, we would not dismiss the whole child. Rather, we would confirm that we liked the child, but were concerned about a specific aspect of the child's behaviour. This was also true of challenges which were made to adults. We made certain that it was the idea and not the person which was being challenged.

Humour often played a large part in which direct challenges were made to other adults. Because of all the team building activities and focusing on personal issues, the staff knew each other quite well. If an unacceptable comment was made, it was usually deflected by a witty remark, which made its point whilst keeping the atmosphere friendly and non-threatening.

Despite the knowledge that they had the right to challenge unacceptable behaviour, several staff preferred to channel their concerns through me. Unfortunately, this did tend to be people who saw themselves as having a 'lower status' than the person they wished to question. Regardless of the ethos we created within the school, it was always people's perceptions of themselves rather than others which were hardest to repudiate. I feel, however, that at least people were airing issues which worried them. Helpers came to me on several occasions concerned about an aspect of a teacher's behaviour. I always listened carefully, discussed what the helper thought should happen to put the matter right, then tactfully approached the teacher. If there was a problem, we then looked at ways to solve it. I always fed back the results of my discussions to the helper. It was important for all staff to realise that matters were not 'swept under the carpet'. Issues were addressed and real results forthcoming.

Managing to be Open

I found that in trying to achieve my aims in promoting equality and ownership amongst staff in the school, I was constantly reviewing my own management style. The structures I have described will only be effective if the management of the school is open and user-friendly and consistent. This did not always prove to be easy. Giving staff an overview of the school, and ownership of the policies within it did mean that I laid myself open for criticism, which, in a way, I had invited. This sometimes felt threatening. For example, the head of one department, which was experiencing difficulties, thought that I should alter my style and dictate to staff in that department. In my opinion this would not have solved the difficulties. I felt that, despite having an overview, the person's criticism was based on a localised perspective of the school. Challenges such as these helped to clarify everyone's thinking and encouraged us to have a broader understanding of each other's perspectives.

Apart from resilience and dedication, an open-management style has certain other requirements.

Negotiable versus non-negotiable

It is imperative to be clear about what is and what is not negotiable as a whole staff. Here, I am reminded of school-based meetings that I attended as a classroom teacher where I realised that seemingly negotiable areas had already been decided upon by the headteacher. I did not feel, therefore, the need to contribute, and so remained silent throughout the meeting. I make it a point in my practice to be very clear about the nature of decision-making. All the points under discussion may not be open to total negotiation, and this needs to be declared. Generally I have found that some principles are not negotiable, whilst procedures often are. For instance, providing equality of opportunity is sacrosanct, whilst ways of achieving this are open to negotiation.

Delegation

Delegating is giving authority to another person to carry out an agreed task. I know of many cases where people have supposedly delegated a task, when what they have actually done is abdicated all responsibility for the outcome and had someone to blame if anything went wrong! If staff believe that this is what is happening, it will come as no surprise to find them reluctant to take responsibility. Clarity is therefore once again very important. There must be an agreed task, agreed aims, an agreed timescale. I must own up to having found delegation difficult. Sometimes I felt it would be easier to do a task myself to save the time and energy involved in explaining it to someone else. Regardless of the amount of trust I had in the delegatee, giving responsibility to a colleague for an important job, for which I was ultimately accountable, was also occasionally quite nerve-racking! Often one has preconceived ideas about what the end result should be. The actual result may be very different in someone else's hands. In setting up delegation channels, it is important to declare that risk-taking and making mistakes are part of the educational process, and that mistakes are not failures. There must also be a 'fail-safe' mechanism which ensures that there are structures in place for feedback and monitoring of the delegated tasks. The bottom line is that delegation is a significant part of professional development.

Celebrating successes

We all know of some headteachers, who seem to delight in patrolling the school and 'catching out' members of staff. Whilst it is important to address unsatisfactory practice, it is also important to celebrate good practice. We worked as a team to integrate this into the way we worked with children. Instead of saying 'don't run', we would say 'Thank you for walking' — a small but significant difference. We also held Good Effort Assemblies each week at which children from different classes, who had perhaps done a very good piece of work, or behaved particularly well would be praised and thanked publicly.

We also praised colleagues' work where appropriate. Aesthetic walks around the school made sure that displays complied with our equal opportunities policy and also served to show teachers the work their colleagues were doing with children. In addition to this, we held meetings in specific teachers' classrooms, giving the teacher the chance to explain the work she or he was doing.

Time management

As is self-evident from the procedures I have set out, achieving objectives as a team takes necessarily longer than 'top down' decision making. An awareness of this, and an ability to manage one's time effectively is essential. Initially, we tended to set unrealistic target dates for certain objectives, which was an issue we had to address. It is vital to allow enough time for the necessary processes to take place, and allow for reflection.

Conclusion

As with any learning experience, there have been expected and unexpected outcomes! One of the most pleasing results of working in the way that we did is that equality of opportunity remained on the agenda all the times. Staff expressed appreciation at having legitimate space to express values, beliefs and ideas. We felt that we had taken a proactive rather than a reactive stance towards equality.

There were, however, times when people felt that their status was being threatened. For instance, a nursery nurse felt that it was inappropriate for her to be working with a group of helpers. This was partially overcome by her also taking part in teaching staff meetings and her involvement in co-planning support staff meetings. It made me aware of the need to address status issues sensitively. However, it was interesting to note that the matter only became an issue when it was a perceived 'higher' status which was apparently under threat.

No management style is flawless. Differences of opinion and conflicts will continue to exist. My open management style helped us to address most of these, but that is not to say that it always provided an immediate solution to every problem. I realised that some conflicts cannot be resolved, but can only be managed. Indeed open management is not the easiest route to take. Giving the power to make decisions to the staff is not without difficulty for a headteacher. What would happen, for instance, if one could not agree to a decision the staff had made? This never actually happened to me, but that did not stop me wondering. Again, being very clear about what is negotiable and what is not should avoid such a problem. The extra time needed to reach some decisions meant that I had to make certain that the outcomes of all meetings and negotiations were well-documented, to provide evidence, for instance, to inspectors that the curriculum and policies were under constant review. Several inspectors, in their turn, expressed their satisfaction at the way we worked.

Open management demands continuous attention and a great deal of stamina. The rewards, however, are tremendous. If aims are clear, the time it takes to achieve them is time well-spent. Working in this way gave us a better understanding and appreciation of each other. We felt that issues such as the isolation of the classroom teacher, who has little time away from the children, were being addressed. Having the structures in place helped us to make overt the fact that we all have racist, sexist, ageist, heterosexist, classist (etc.) values. This made it easier for us to challenge our own prejudices, and deal with the problems they may raise. Overall, I believe the staff felt more valued, and I feel we were able to bring about tangible change for the better within the school.

18 Equal Opportunities and Sexuality

PAUL PATRICK and HELENA BURKE

This article challenges the view that attitudes towards sexuality might be too difficult or contentious an area to tackle in equal opportunities work, particularly at primary level. The authors show that young children are already acquiring homophobic attitudes which will have long reaching adverse effects, both on themselves and others. They suggest some starting points for work on attitudes to sexuality at primary level, and argue that if a school is to develop an equal opportunities policy, then this policy will defeat its own aims if it does not address all areas of discrimination.

Introduction: Breaking the Conspiracy of Silence

'All of us whether we know it or not have lesbian and gay children, friends, relatives or colleagues. And when they are teased, bullied, harassed, sacked from jobs, beaten up or even driven to suicide or murdered because they love someone of their own sex perhaps we should ask ourselves isn't it time for all of us to do something about it? And aren't families and schools, the very grass roots of society where attitudes are formed, the best places to start?' (Bendel, 1991)

The above quote is not taken from a radical educational document but from *Living*, a family magazine, that, despite the fact it assumes all its readers to be heterosexual, recognises the importance of an issue that many schools have yet to take on board.

The aim of this chapter is to argue that issues of sexuality must be included in any meaningful equal opportunities policy and to suggest some possible starting points for work in the primary school. As teachers ourselves we have been involved in the development of such policies both within schools and teacher training.

Some people may argue that primary age children are too young to understand issues of lesbian/gay sexuality, but many primary teachers will know that children have 'information' picked up from the home and playground. By a very young age they have learnt the unacceptability of lesbian/gay lifestyles. A primary teacher tells of a five-year-old regaling her classmates with stories of 'the queers who live upstairs'.

Carol Ackroyd, a lesbian mother and educationalist, makes this point: 'From those very first days of school, they clearly recognise the negative value judgements attached to our lives' (Ackroyd, 1987).

During the period that this chapter was being written one of the authors happened to pass a holiday playgroup. Two young boys were standing on a rather high wall about to jump off. One invited the other to hold hands while they did this. The other replied, 'No, I'm not a poof'. They were five or six.

Well before secondary school age children learn the vocabulary of homophobia. Jenny Scoffield, head of Humanities in a London primary school states:

> 'In both the playground and the classroom the use of words like "poof", "battyman", "lezzie" etc. are routinely used by even very young children when they think they can get away with it. I think it is as much the teacher's job to challenge this sort of abuse and explain why it is unacceptable as it is to deal with racist and sexist abuse.'

Such attitudes derive from the home, the media and the playground. We don't have the choice as to whether children know or don't know about homosexuality, we can only decide whether their picture is based on prejudice or reality.

The negative attitudes frequently expressed in school have particular consequences for those pupils who have lesbian/gay parents or other relatives, and for the future lives of pupils who choose to be lesbian/gay themselves. Children of lesbian/gay parents have to cope with a gap between the reality of their lives and that which school presents as 'normal'. Carol Ackroyd again:

> 'Their drawing books and stories present a censored version of their lives; they deal with the lack of a father by destroying him in a car crash; other central characters in their lives don't feature at all.'

Under such circumstances it is hardly surprising that these children find school a difficult and unhappy place to be. A child of lesbian parents comments:

> 'For all children who don't come from conventional families ... which have a married mummy and daddy who are definitely heterosexual,

school never really feels as though it belongs to you. The curriculum, the teachers, and most of the kids all seem so adamantly heterosexual. There is nothing for us to do if we want to survive in this environment except to pretend, cover up, be silent.' (Bahaire, 1987)

As for those pupils who grow up to be lesbian/gay, they suffer abuse, fear and isolation, with schools frequently compounding rather than ameliorating the problem. Their position, and schools' responses to it have been documented by Lorraine Trenchard and Hugh Warren:

'I found that at school I didn't know what gay was, and I felt very alone. When I did eventually get to know what the feeling I had was, I was frightened because those who were gay or supposed to look gay, were picked on.'

'I do not remember homosexuality/lesbianism coming up at all in sex education or in discussions on relationships.'

'I really did think I was the only young gay. That's what made me take the tablets; attempt suicide.' (Trenchard & Warren, 1984)

The same research has shown that one in five young lesbians and gay man have attempted suicide. According to Paul Farmer of the Samaritans 'The number of young people who attempt suicide is much higher than the national average. Undoubtedly those who are adapting to or questioning their own sexual orientation run a higher risk and this is something we're very concerned about' (quoted in Bendel, 1991).

However, it is not just these two groups of children who would benefit from an equal opportunities policy which includes sexuality. If we argue that all children benefit from anti-racist and anti-sexist education, then all children must benefit from an education which challenges the fear and prejudice that so often surround issues of sexuality. For far too long the issue of young people's attitude to their own and others' sexuality has been ignored by schools. Yet sexuality remains a major component of all our lives. It is surely time that schools realised the educational necessity of breaking this 'conspiracy of silence' for the benefit of all our pupils and society as a whole.

Developing a Comprehensive Policy

Once a school staff have agreed to include sexuality in an equal opportunities policy the next step is to turn principle into policy. In our experience, by far the most effective way to do this is to ensure that equal opportunities is treated in a holistic fashion, by the creation of a generalised statement of intent which makes particular reference to the full range of equal opportunities issues. This enables a school to develop a unified approach to prejudice and discrimination.

One school that has taken this approach argues:

'From the beginning it was clear that the school needed an overall policy statement that would encompass a commitment to all sections of the community and not merely emphasise those areas of equal opportunity that were considered politically expedient at the time. The idea of 'equal opportunity for some' was seen as a betrayal of the comprehensive ideal that promised equal access to education for all.' (Stop the Clause Group, 1989)

The policy evolved from this is for a secondary school, but we believe the general principles underlying it are equally applicable to primary schools. Many of the attitudes it is designed to challenge take root early in children's lives.

... We recognise that many members of the school may experience prejudice and harassment both within the school and outside. The school therefore commits itself fully to a policy of challenging prejudice and discrimination on the grounds of:

Ability	*Age*
Class	*Disability*
Gender	*HIV Positive and AIDS status*
Language	*Physical appearance*
Racial, ethnic or national	*Religion*
origin	*Sexual orientation*
Status	

Such a policy requires commitment from each member of the school community and the acceptance of a code of conduct which:

(a) encourages respect for the individual;

(b) encourages collective action to challenge prejudice and the structures that perpetuate it;

(c) challenges stereotyped images and, in their place, promotes positive images;

(d) declares as unacceptable any language, action or belief that is prejudice or which encourages prejudice in others.

It is the duty of all members of the school community to uphold this policy, even where it may differ from their own personal beliefs.

This provided the school with a clear statement of intent, which could form the basis of consultation with parents, governors and teaching and support staff. The importance of such consultation cannot be underestimated. Nor need it be seen as particularly problematic. Our experience has been that when issues have been presented as part of a coherent package for the benefit of all pupils and open and full discussion is encouraged, active support is frequently achieved. This holistic approach avoids the labelling of sexuality as a 'controversial issue' which frequently arouses unnecessary fears. Rather it allows the exploration of this issue in conjunction with other areas of equal opportunity.

Primary School Practice

The special relationship developed between primary schools and parents can provide an excellent opportunity for developing policy and practice in relation to sexuality. Teachers often wrongly assume that parents and governors shy away from such issues. We have found the opposite to be true.

Once a comprehensive equal opportunities policy has been established it provides the opportunity for the school to work on issues of sexuality and obliges all school employees to play their part in this as 'it is the duty of all members of the school community to uphold this policy, *even where it may differ from their own personal beliefs*'. This will obviously include significant work falling within the remit of sex education but more fundamental will be the task of challenging heterosexism across the curriculum (i.e. the disparagement of lesbian and gay lifestyles through the assumption that heterosexuality is a more valid option).

In the area of sex education it would be important to get away from the notion that 'sex equals reproduction' and to include references to lesbian and gay sexuality where relevant. The National Curriculum Council Guidance no. 5 on Health Education says that sex education should provide knowledge about the nature of sexuality and relationships, as well as about the processes of reproduction.

Some of the ways in which heterosexism can be challenged within the primary school curriculum are:

(a)   The inclusion of lesbian/gay people as part of the community and as alternatives to the nuclear family. Work on the family should include acknowledgement of the range of family groupings that exist: extended families, nuclear families, one parent families, lesbian and gay families.

(b)   Positive images of lesbian/gay people alongside those of other individuals and community groups acknowledging the homosexuality of famous and successful lesbian and gay people. E.g. Justin Fashanu, footballer; Martina Navratalova, tennis player; Florence Nightingale, founder of modern nursing; Shaka, leader of the Zulu Nation against Boer and British invasions of Southern Africa. This should happen in the same way that any good teacher would ensure their work presented positive images of black people, women and people with disabilities.

(c)   The inclusion in the school/classroom libraries of books which depict gay/lesbian families (see references).

(d)   Challenging anti-gay/lesbian remarks and developing educational and disciplinary procedures to deal with them.

Jenny Scoffield again:

'I was taking a group of top juniors and organising them into groups, which were named after colours. A boy I put into the "pink" group said, "I don't want to go in there that's a poof's group". I immediately stopped the class and asked him what he meant. He said that pink was a colour associated with "poofs" and therefore he didn't want to join that group. I first talked to the class about the use of language, equating the use of the word "poof" with terms of racist and sexist abuse, pointing out that the school would not accept such language. I then explained to the whole class the origin of gay men's use of the pink triangle as an affirmation of their sexuality and an expression of pride and remembrance. (It was originally the symbol that Nazi Germany made the half million homosexuals whom they took into the concentration camps and murdered wear to distinguish them from other prisoners.) The boy agreed to go into the pink group.'

This example gives us a model for such intervention:

(1)   Use the issue as a learning experience for the whole class.

(2)   Make it clear that it is the school that finds the situation unacceptable, so that it cannot be dismissed as the idiosyncrasy of the individual teacher.

(3)   Where possible provide an educational input so that the pupils understand as clearly as possible the issue that is raised.

As one parent states:

'I want primary teachers to inform children about alternatives to the nuclear family, and to integrate this into all their work concerning home backgrounds. I want them to use the words "lesbian" and "gay" and to present them as a valid personal and political identity (and not a sexual act).'

'I want them to discuss prejudice with the children.'

'I want this for all children ... but particularly for the ones who will become heterosexual, to encourage them to take responsibility for challenging heterosexism.' (Ackroyd, 1987)

Government Legislation and Advice

Recently there has been much discussion about the legal position of schools that wish to develop the type of policy outlined above, and National Government has increased both legislation and advice to schools about this area.

The first major reference to the treatment of lesbian and gay lifestyles from a National Government source comes in the HMI document *Health Education from 5 to 16*, one of a series of Department of Education and Science curriculum documents. It states:

'Given the openness with which homosexuality is treated within society now it is almost bound to arise as an issue in one area or another of the school's curriculum ... Therefore it needs to be dealt with objectively and seriously ...' (DES, 1986)

The importance of the statement is in its recognition of a clear change in social attitude to which it is necessary that schools respond. It goes on to remind teachers that the issues must be dealt with sensitively, pointing out the wide range of attitudes and responses that the subject still provokes. This is a view with which we would concur.

The development of policy in this area, as in all areas of equal opportunity, demands sensitive and open discussion of all the issues involved with parents, governors, pupils and colleagues. The role of the governing body is of specific importance where such a policy may effect the teaching of sex education within a school. Section 46 of the Education (No.2) Act 1986 requires that:

'The local education authority by whom any county, voluntary or special school is maintained, and the governing body and the head teacher of the school, shall take such steps as are reasonably practical to secure that where sex education is given to any registered pupils at the school it is given in such a manner as to encourage those pupils to have due regard for moral considerations and the value of family life.'

The DES circular 11/87 which provided schools with additional advice on sex education goes on to say:

'The Secretary of State considers the aims of a programme of sex education should be to present the facts in an objective and balanced manner so as to enable pupils to comprehend the range of sexual attitudes and behaviour in present day society: to know what is and what is not legal; to consider their own attitudes, and to make informed, reasoned and responsible decisions about the attitudes they will adopt both while they are at school and in adulthood.' (DES, 1987)

It is our belief that it would be impossible to achieve these laudable aims without the inclusion of sexuality in an equal opportunities policy and the development of the sort of work outlined above.

The other piece of legislation which relates to this work is Section 28 of the Local Government Act (1988) which states:

A local authority shall not:

(a) intentionally promote homosexuality or publish material with the intention of promoting homosexuality.

(b) promote the teaching in any maintained school of the acceptability of homosexuality as a pretended family relationship.

The section was originally a private members bill that was then included by the Government within their legislation on local authorities. The vagueness of its wording and the lack of evidence from those proposing the section that such promotion had ever occurred has meant that both educational and legal opinion consider it to have no effect upon the work suggested in this chapter. In fact Mrs Thatcher reassured those concerned about the possible consequences of the section with the words:

'The Government is against discrimination in any form, and it is no part of our intention in supporting Clause 28 to remove the rights of homosexuals; ... they are entitled to receive the same council services on the same basis as everyone else. There is nothing in the clause that would damage this right ...' (Thatcher, 1988)

Michael Barnes QC, when providing legal opinion on the Section, stated:

'It is important to observe that this section does not preclude teachers from dealing in a honest and objective way with homosexuality in the classroom. For, in the first place, the section is not aimed at teachers at all. Secondly ... nothing in the new section requires teachers to act contrary to the welfare of their individual pupils.' (quoted in Stop the Clause Group, 1989)

It is obvious that it is no part of a teacher's role to 'promote homosexuality' any more than it is to 'promote heterosexuality'. It is however, a teacher's duty to promote tolerance, understanding and respect for self and others through the presentation of appropriate information and the facilitating of discussion in a supportive framework. Nothing in Section 28 prevents that from taking place.

Personal Perspectives and Practice

To take on such issues has implications for staff. For many teachers this will involve looking at your own attitudes and confronting your own prejudice. This can best be done through the inclusion in teacher training of appropriate work raising lesbian and gay issues in education and supportive in-service training for practising teachers. It is the professional obligation of all teachers to raise their understanding of these issues if they are to facilitate work that allows children to develop a healthy attitude to sexuality.

When beginning this work you will need to be aware of the range of reactions from pupils that you may encounter. Pupils from lesbian/gay families who have previously felt unable to discuss this at school, may choose to confide in you. Some primary age pupils will be aware of their developing sexuality and will wish to discuss it with you. Other pupils may be very reticent to discuss the issues at all, or may be particularly hostile. This should not necessarily be seen as lack of interest or as a picture of their true opinions. Many pupils will want to distance themselves from some aspects of the discussion and they should be allowed to do so. You may also be questioned on your own sexuality and your response to this needs careful thought. In discussion with both heterosexual and lesbian and gay teachers, we have found one of the most useful strategies is to use this question as a springboard for discussion. 'Would it make a difference?' provides much more space for educational debate than replying 'No', if you happen to be heterosexual, which invariably closes down further discussion.

If you happen to be lesbian/gay you will need to think very carefully about whether you choose to declare your sexuality at all and if so, when and how. Clearly your response would depend upon the ethos and commitment of your own school and the extent to which you feel you will gain the support of staff, parents and governors for such a move. It is a decision that should only be taken after much thought. Our experience has shown that in schools where there are openly lesbian and gay staff the benefits to pupils are immense, as they provide positive role models for all pupils, their presence initiates and informs discussion and shows lesbian and gay people to be 'just like anyone else'. However this does not mean that the development of these issues should be seen as the province of lesbian and gay staff, rather they are the responsibility of the whole school.

We have argued that it is impossible to talk truly of equal opportunities in anything but a holistic way, with sexuality playing an essential part in this process. If equal opportunities in education is to mean anything, if we're not actively to deceive children, if lesbian and gay people are not to continue to suffer and heterosexuals to remain in ignorance of the range and validity of human sexuality, then everyone involved in education must commit themselves fully to real equal opportunities for all. Everyone must begin a process of negotiation and education similar to that set out above. Our experience has shown that where all issues of equal opportunities are negotiated in an honest and open manner, exciting and important advances are made for the benefit of pupils, parents, governors and staff.

References

Ackroyd, C. (1987) What do we want from primary schools?, *GEN Magazine*, March.
Bahaire, E. (1987) My mum's a lesbian, *GEN Magazine*, March.
Bendel, L. (1991) Homosexuality: What every parent should know. *Living Magazine*, April.
DES (1986) *Health Education from 5 to 16: An HME Series* (DES Curriculum Matters 6). London: HMSO.
DES (1987) *Circular 11/87 on Sex Education*. London: DES.
National Curriculum Council (1990) *National Curriculum Council Guidance No. 5: Health Education*. York: NCC.
Stop the Clause Group (1989) *Section 28: A Guide for Schools, Teachers and Governors*. London: ALTARF.
Thatcher, M. (1988) Letter to a constituent, 3 March. Quoted in Stop the Clause Group *Section 28: A Guide for Schools, Teachers and Governors. London: ALTARF*.
Trenchard, L. and Warren, H. (1984) Something to tell you. In H. Warren (ed.) *Talking about School*. London Gay Teenage Group.

Appendix: A List of Children's Fiction

Here is a short and quite personal list of children's books compiled by Hilary Claire. The list is divided into three sections: the first (and shortest) section contains those books which deal specifically with children growing up with gay or lesbian parents. The other two contain children's book which challenge stereotypical images — often in quite subtle ways — and offer alternative, positive role models for boys and girls. Several focus on supportive friendships and caring relationships between children and many of the books feature black families.

The books range from picture books for the early years to fiction for good readers at the top of the primary school. Unfortunately, the titles are sometimes misleading, for example, *Willie Is Not the Hugging Kind* is a wonderful picture book about a small black boy who discovers the importance and power of showing his feelings. Most of the titles listed (including the foreign imports) can be obtained through Letterbox Library, Unit 2D,

Leroy House, 426 Essex Road, London N1 3QP. Letterbox has an annotated and illustrated catalogue.

Section 1: Growing Up With Gay or Lesbian Parents

Elwin, R. and Paulse, M. (1990) *Asha's Mums.* Toronto: Women's Press.
Langoulant, A. (1991) *Everybody's Different.* London: Blackie.
Severance, J. (1979) *When Megan Went Away.* California: Lollipop Power Books.
Willhoite, M. (1990) Daddy's Roommate. Alyson Publishers.

Section 2: Books With Girls as the Main Character

Bradman, T. (1989) *Sam the Girl Detective* (and other titles in this series). Yearling
    Books.
Caines, J. (1980) *Window Wishing.* Harper & Row.
De Poix, C. (1973) *Jo, Flo and Yolanda.* California: Lollipop Power Books.
Dowling, P. (1991) *Splodger.* ABC Books.
Gleeson, L. (1988) *I am Susannah.* Australia: Bluegum.
Hoffman, M. (1991) *Amazing Grace.* Frances Lincoln.
Homan, D. *In Christine's Toolbox.* California: Lollipop Power Books.
Kaye, G. (1991) *Snowgirl.* Banana Books (Heinemann).
MacDonald, M. (1991) *The Pirate Queen.* Orchard Books.
Oram, H. (1992) *Reckless Ruby.* Andersen Press.
Pfanner, L. *Louise Builds a House.* William Collins.
Woodson, J. (1990) *Last Summer with Maizon.* Heinemann.

Section 3: Books With Boys as the Main Character

Bogart, J. (1990) *Daniel's Dog.* Scholastic.
Browene, A. (1991) *Willy and Hugh.* Julia MacRae.
De Paula, T. (1990) *Oliver Button is a Sissy.* Harcourt Brace Jovanovitch.
Durham Barrett, J. (1989) *Willie's Not the Hugging Kind.* Harper Trophy.
Fine, A. (1989) *Bill's New Frock.* Mammoth.
Graham, B. (1987) *Crusher is Coming.* Collins Picture Lions.
Mack, B. (1979) *Jesse's Dream Skirt.* California: Lollipop Power Books.
Pitts Walter, M. (1990) *Little Sister, Big Trouble.* Simon & Schuster.
Robinson, C. (1991) *Sam and the Swans.* Viking.
Zolotow, C. *William's Doll.* Harper Trophy.

71   15